## MORE FROM A BOOK APAR

**Working the Command Line**
*Remy Sharp*

**Pricing Design**
*Dan Mall*

**Get Ready for CSS Grid Layout**
*Rachel Andrew*

Visit abookapart.com for our full list of titles.

Publisher: Jeffrey Zeldman
Designer: Jason Santa Maria
Executive Director: Katel LeDû
Managing Editor: Tina Lee
Editor: Tina Lee
Technical Editors: Marc Edwards, Gus Mueller
Copyeditor: Caren Litherland
Proofreader: Katel LeDû
Compositor: Rob Weychert
Ebook Producer: Ron Bilodeau

ISBN: 978-1-937557-51-5

A Book Apart
New York, New York
http://abookapart.com

10 9 8 7 6 5 4 3 2 1

# TABLE OF CONTENTS

# FOREWORD

EARLY IN MY CAREER, I worked as a graphic designer dealing mostly with print. Getting color right wasn't easy, but it was completely under my control as a designer, because I could target the output. I'd go to the print shop, examine the first copies off the press, and if they looked good, I'd feel confident that the whole print run would look the same.

Now with digital designs, we have no control over the output platform. Thousands of different displays are in use, and our work might appear on any or all of them.

Getting colors right? Here are a few scenarios: a graphic image and CSS background color should match exactly, but they don't. Or they do match on some devices, but not on others. Or they don't match on *any* devices, and good luck identifying the cause. It's enough to drive one back to vintage Macs that only display black and white.

When I encounter a color mismatch, I deal with it like so (a tactic I suspect many of you take too): fiddle with various color settings in image editing software and source code until it works out, and hope to remember the magic recipe the next time the problem happens. (There is always a next time.)

Craig did something different. In this book, he takes a step back to truly understand how color management actually works. Better yet, he shares that complex knowledge in a clear, immediate way. He tells us not just what to do, but *why*. Craig effortlessly guides us through the principles and practice of color management; as I read, I kept thinking, *Well, that's actually pretty simple*—a big realization given I'd treated the subject as a dark art for fifteen years.

Color computing has never been easy. Our computers are almost unimaginably more powerful than those from years past, but designers and programmers have never stopped pushing the limits of our hardware. The goal has always been the same: to make what appears on screen look as good as it possibly can. Thanks to Craig, it's now a little easier to achieve.

—**John Gruber**

# INTRODUCTION

STEP INTO THE TELEVISION SECTION of any electronics store, and you'll see how widely colors can vary from screen to screen. You'll see how many colors are generated by the exact same red, green, and blue (RGB) values—each TV gets the same digital broadcast, yet there's a huge range in the displayed images. Color management lets us describe those differences, and correct them.

I dug into the guts of color management when I wrote xScope, my development tool for sampling and measuring colors. Back then, I didn't really understand Photoshop's mechanisms for handling color; I went and set some levers, which worked most of the time. But when xScope's colors appeared one way in Safari and another in Chrome, I didn't know which controls were responsible. I *did* know the problem was with color management.

If you've been in the business awhile, this confusion over color probably sounds familiar, and I began this book as a means to share what I've learned in understanding my color issues. In the coming chapters, I'll run through some experiments to show how color works, why colors shift in different environments, and ways to keep those colors consistent.

As conscientious developers, we want to create things that look good anywhere. Just as responsive design lets layouts adapt to variety, color management lets colors and images adjust to their device and presentation.

With knowledge of color management, you'll gain more confidence as you adjust the settings in your image editor, *and* you'll be able to create products that look better for more people. Everyone wins.

1

# COPING WITH COLORS

You just got a gig to design a website for an optometrist, Dr. Eyeful. Sweet!

The doctor wants you to use his two favorite colors: red and purple. (Bonus points if you include a "site" and "sight" pun in the tagline.)

You've been developing sites since the days of web-safe color palettes. By picking red, green, and blue (RGB) values of `(255, 0, 0)` and `(102, 0, 204)`, you'll satisfy the doctor's branding requirements while working with tried-and-true colors. Of course, you're careful to use those exact color specifications in both your Photoshop document and CSS styles.

But when you load the page in your browser, you see a weird color shift in the header (**FIG 1.1**).

Other browsers show a similar color shift, until you look at the page on your tablet—and it's perfect! What the heck?

After a bit of surfing, you find a site that recommends specifying something called sRGB in Photoshop. You don't know *exactly* what that means, but you tweak things and save a new graphic file. It fixes the problem in Safari, but the color is still off in Chrome. No matter what you do, you can't get the CSS and image colors to match.

This inconsistency bugs you. The doctor may have questionable taste in colors, but his eyesight is perfect. He's going to see these shifts and ask what's happening.

Problem is, you really have no clue.

## WHAT IS COLOR MANAGEMENT?

At the most basic level, *color management* is a way to specify the range of colors a device can represent.

Many designers and developers, including your author, have found ways to wrangle color without truly understanding the underlying technology. We've leaned on simple standards, choosing three bytes of data for the primary colors of light: red, green, and blue. When we specified R=255, G=0, and B=0, we expected—and could expect—to see red on our displays. We could pretty much ignore anything else about color, whether we were designing for the web or a native app.

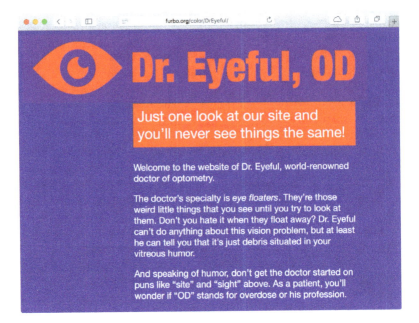

furbo.org/color/DrEyeful/

# Dr. Eyeful, OD

**Just one look at our site and you'll never see things the same!**

Welcome to the website of Dr. Eyeful, world-renowned doctor of optometry.

The doctor's specialty is *eye floaters*. They're those weird little things that you see until you try to look at them. Don't you hate it when they float away? Dr. Eyeful can't do anything about this vision problem, but at least he can tell you that it's just debris situated in your vitreous humor.

And speaking of humor, don't get the doctor started on puns like "site" and "sight" above. As a patient, you'll wonder if "OD" stands for overdose or his profession.

**FIG 1.1**: The site header is an eyeful. What's worse, the colors are shifting.

This worked for a time, but as you saw with Dr. Eyeful, our basic RGB values don't translate the same way across devices. To find out why, let's take a quick trip through history.

## Coping with too many choices

Color management isn't new. Photographers and print designers have dealt with calibrating colors for decades. It all started when people took images captured on film and output them on paper with ink. Sounds straightforward, right? But you had different kinds of film stock, along with paper weight and finish. The variety of inks was astounding; the huge collection of Pantone colors, for instance, got its start in the 1960s as colored liquids.

Such technological diversity made it hard to keep imagery consistent as it made its way from the camera lens to the printed page. Photographers, designers, and printers knew they couldn't rely solely on an RGB or a CMYK color space to get consistent results. Their workflow included another component, which profiled the color capabilities of their equipment—and adjusted colors accordingly. (This component was a complex mathematical model based on the human eye: a color profile. We'll get to this soon.)

We face the same scenario now, the same variety in technology. The digital sensor on a cheap cell phone camera can't capture as many colors as a high-end, pricey DSLR. Similarly, an LCD display from only a few years ago looks absolutely horrible when compared to the Retina display on an iMac. OLED technology on wristwatches is a new animal entirely.

If you want your reds, greens, and blues to look right across browsers or apps, you need to pay attention to how you specify colors in your tools. While you often won't have much choice about how color is processed by a platform, you will get unpredictable results if you ignore the requirements of whatever environment you're working in—which is what happened with Dr. Eyeful's website.

Understanding color management yields dividends. You'll ensure branding and other color elements in your interface look the best they can. And think how many elements are involved in a website—all the interface graphics, hero images, and other bits—wouldn't it be great if you could reuse those assets, without modification, in a mobile app?

You can, once you know how your workflow manages color and your target platforms present the images. As a first step, let's examine how colors got their start on our computers.

## Old-fashioned color

In the late 1970s, color began to appear on computer displays. These early machines had little memory—sometimes as small as 4,096 characters total. Processors were also limited, and accessed memory eight bits at a time, giving programmers a minimum value of 0 and a maximum value of 255.

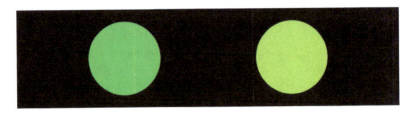

FIG 1.2: Two green bulbs produce different colors.

Although machines have become much more powerful, specifying color with eight bits has stayed with us: three RGB channels together produce 16,777,216 unique colors, a range that closely matches what our eyes can see. Some apps use 16-bit color, but this extended range mostly benefits editing images.

We'll use 8-bit values throughout this book; to get more accurate color, we'll add another type of data.

### Green light bulbs

Imagine we have two green light bulbs, made by two manufacturers.

When the bulbs are fully lit, even if you're affected by certain forms of color blindness, you can tell the colors differ slightly (**FIG 1.2**). This is unsurprising, since the manufacturers used separate processes and materials.

But your computer isn't so smart. All it knows is that G=0 means the bulb is off, G=127 is at half brightness, and G=255 is fully on.

Now imagine two displays made with these light bulbs. I have the one on the left, and you have the one on the right. When I specify G=255, I see the color on the left. But when I send you a file with that G=255, you see the color on the right.

Whoops. It might seem minor, but it wouldn't be to a client like Starbucks, Heineken, or John Deere, which takes green very seriously. You could lose hours perfecting the green on your screen and have the CEO see something else. That's just the tip of the iceberg: every customer who visits your client's site can have a completely different light bulb.

As photographers and print designers learned, we can't solely rely on the values for primary colors. We also need information, or a *color profile*, from the manufacturer that explains how they display the color green.

## COLOR PROFILES

Anything that can capture or display an image—your camera, your monitor, etc.—has a set of values that describes the range of colors available for use. This set of data is the color profile, and it comes in a format defined by the International Color Consortium (ICC).

Creating a profile involves *a lot* of science. If you're a manufacturer of green light bulbs, you'll take an expensive piece of equipment, a color spectrophotometer, to measure the amount of visible light produced at different color wavelengths. You then use that data to generate a mathematical model—the profile, which is specific to the device: my iMac display profile would look terrible on your MacBook.

Some manufacturers choose to use a standard profile for their bulbs. Two of the most popular are *Adobe RGB* and *standard RGB* (sRGB):

· Adobe introduced its profile in 1998 to represent CMYK printer colors on an RGB display. It's a favorite among photographers, because its wide range of colors produces better images in post-processing.
· Made around the same time, sRGB mimics typical viewing conditions in a home or office, with a smaller range of colors (making it cheaper and easier to produce). Its ubiquity makes it the color space for defining web standards.

Cameras often support Adobe RGB (or ProPhoto, the color space developed by Kodak), while many displays (like that bargain LCD at the electronics store) conform to sRGB.

Let's see what these two standard profiles look like (**FIG 1.3**).

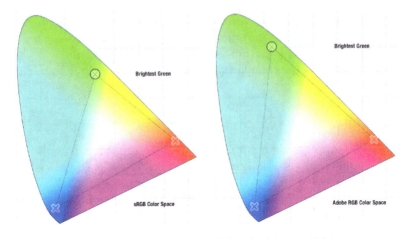

**FIG 1.3:** The color ranges of two profiles: sRGB (left) and Adobe RGB (right).

The curved shape with a flat side represents all the colors the human eye can see—it never changes. Each triangle represents a color profile; the X-corners are fully saturated red, green, and blue.

The black circle marks the brightest green the profile can produce. It's like our green light bulbs: sRGB's green has a yellow tint, while Adobe's is closer to the ideal color our eyes see. (As you'll find out in a moment, the weird shape springs from our physiology!)

The size, or *gamut*, of each triangle reflects the range of possible colors. The larger triangle, Adobe RGB, has a *wider gamut* (which is why the profile is so popular among photographers).

Keen observers will note black isn't present. That's because we cheated a bit and showed only two dimensions. When we add color saturation, the curved shape lies on its side and a fully saturated white appears as a peak, with black as a base (**FIG 1.4**).

That pointy shape is everything our computers need to take the raw numeric values in our files and display them so we all see a similar color.

FIG 1.4: sRGB color profile with saturation as a third dimension.

## A profile to fit your eye

There's no getting around it: color management is complex. At its core, after all, is a numerical model for the human eye.

It doesn't help that behind this heavy-duty science is a slew of acronyms. Let me take a minute to break down a few names and concepts that led to my first "aha!" moment in learning about color management. First up, the Commission Internationale de l'Eclairage, the global authority on light and color. If you don't speak French, that's International Commission on Illumination—but everyone refers to this group as CIE.

Our retinas contain three types of cone cells that detect light. Each type senses a different part of the color spectrum: blues at short wavelengths, greens in the middle, and reds at longer wavelengths. The curved boundary in the shapes you saw is a plot of chromatic wavelengths visible to our eyes.

Our brains take stimuli from these cells and combine them to give us color perception (and the official term, *tristimulus*.) The scientists at CIE codified this biology into a mathematical model called *CIEXYZ* in 1931.

Over the next 45 years, understanding of the human eye improved. Researchers found that somewhere between the optic nerve and the brain, stimuli are categorized according to degrees of lightness, red/green, and blue/yellow. This led to a second key color model, *CIELAB*.

Don't let the old age of CIELAB and CIEXYZ trick you: both are still the standards to put your eye's behavior into numbers our computers can process:

- Since it takes into account how our brains perceive color, a LAB color space is better at reproducing tones and relative color values. LAB is ideal for color created with inks.
- The XYZ color space is based on the eye's response to stimulation across the visible light spectrum. This works well for specifying an exact color, even though it ignores that our vision isn't completely uniform. XYZ is ideal for devices that emit light, like a computer display.

## The eye's color profile makes everything work

Phew: you've dipped your toe into the complicated waters of color science! The important thing to know is both CIE color spaces are device-independent: their only dependence is on our bodies (which thankfully don't change as fast as technology).

The eye's freedom from hardware is crucial to moving colors between profiles.

Converting directly between devices would be painful: every device would need to know about every other device in the world. Your display would need to know about all kinds of cameras before it could work with photos. Same with your printer and editing software. Think about how many models of cameras, printers, and displays exist, and you'll see this situation would soon become unwieldy.

Instead, we base conversion on the eye, so each device only needs to specify how to transform color to and from the eye's color space (FIG 1.5). The raw numeric color values differ depending on the document or device, but they all look the same. Because of their central role, the CIE models are referred to as *profile connection spaces.*

You'll probably never use CIEXYZ or CIELAB directly, but every time a pixel moves from one place to another, one of the eye's color spaces will play a part in making sure that pixel looks its best.

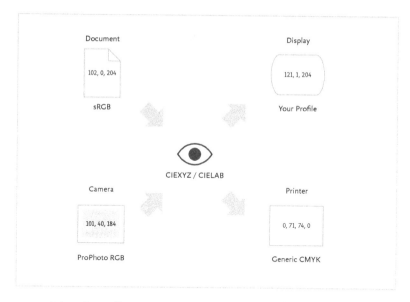

FIG 1.5: Using color profiles, the eye perceives the same color for different raw values.

## Profiles are everywhere

Color profiles are relatively small pieces of data, which makes them easy to embed in image files and design documents. A file with this profile information can be handled predictably by any editor or presentation mechanism (including things as diverse as printers and web browsers).

File formats that can embed profiles include popular ones for web images (JPEG, PNG, SVG) and documents (PSD, PDF). Digital negatives (DNG) allow profiles too, and color profiles may even someday become part of your CSS.

The color profile information can also be stored in a separate file. These files typically accompany hardware peripherals like displays, printers, and cameras, where it'd be impractical to embed the data.

Editors and other products that manipulate design use a color profile that describes the range of colors available while you're creating artwork. This profile is often referred to as the *working space*. Some apps, like Photoshop, let you choose the working space. Other apps use a predefined color space, usually a standard one like sRGB.

If you're curious, you can explore all the color profiles installed on your Mac using the ColorSync Utility in the Applications > Utilities folder. Under Profiles, you'll see a long list, sourced from Apple, Adobe, the display manufacturer, and many others. When you select a profile, its graphic representation appears, along with other details.

## THE DISPLAYS THEY ARE A-CHANGIN'

While the eye stays steady, let's now peek at the device side. Displays have reached the point where human eyes can't determine individual pixels—increasing the resolution has no benefit. The next frontier lies in color depth, making our images more vibrant. And we're already there, in two ways: pixels that have a wider range of values, and color spaces that boast larger gamuts.

As an example, iMac computers from 2015 onward support ten bits of color per pixel. These new screens can display a gradient with thousands of unique values, versus regular displays with only a couple hundred values. Where you once saw banding and other artifacts, you'll now see smooth transitions between colors.

Along with these superpixels, these displays also show a much wider range of colors (FIG 1.6). Instead of the standard sRGB profile from the computer industry, Apple is employing a new profile from the motion picture world: *DCI P3*.

DCI stands for Digital Cinema Initiatives, a collective body of six major film studios. In 2007, DCI created a set of specs to standardize digital cinema systems and ensure uniform quality in theaters. Manufacturers like Apple are now adapting the DCI standard for desktop computers and mobile devices—Apple's Display P3 color space uses the same wide gamut as your local movie theater, but adjusts for the brighter viewing conditions in your home or office.

New profiles mean changes to the way information is displayed; Apple is adding new features to its web browser and

**FIG 1.6:** The white area depicts the additional colors DCI P3 can display over sRGB.

providing support for color profiles on mobile devices. Other manufacturers will follow suit in the coming years—and as you'll see in later chapters, you'll have more P3 in your life and less sRGB.

When sRGB isn't the only game in town, we may wind up with more goofs like the one on Dr. Eyeful's site. Luckily, with your grasp of color management, you'll be in a solid position to avoid these problems!

## UGLY FOR A REASON

Throughout this book, I'll specify colors in the 0–255 range, the 8-bit convention that conveniently fits all tools and documents. While the colors aren't pretty (they might even sear your retinas after prolonged exposure), I've chosen them on purpose:

- Red (255, 0, 0) and purple (102, 0, 204) will push the color gamut of most displays; colors are more likely to shift when they're at the monitor's physical limits. (They're also responsible for a nice paycheck from Dr. Eyeful.)
- The values of brown (123, 45, 67) and blue (12, 34, 56) are consecutive sequences. It'll be easy to spot any color shifts: just look for out-of-place digits.

To that end, you'll need a tool to measure the color values in various color spaces. On macOS, the Digital Color Meter is in the Applications > Utilities folder. Since you'll use it to measure colors in the 0-255 range, make sure to select View > Display Values > as Decimal.

Alternatively, you can use xScope to color-check; the most recent version supports color spaces under the Loupe > Working Color Space menu.

(Those of you working on Windows will have a tougher time with some examples: only Windows 10 supports color management, and it isn't enabled by default. Photoshop for Windows handles color the same as the Mac version, but popular screen-sampling tools like Eyedropper, Pixie, and ColorPix don't support color spaces.)

In some of the screenshots, you'll see "huey D65." That's my monitor, which was calibrated with Pantone's Huey colorimeter. A colorimeter measures the light produced by a display and automatically creates a color profile—this profile is more accurate than the generic one that comes with your display, since it can be tuned to ambient lighting.

You can also manually calibrate your screen on a Mac by using the Color tab of the Display panel in System Preferences. After selecting "Calibrate...," you'll be guided through a process that will likely improve the images on your monitor.

## ONWARD

We've zipped through an overview of the past, present, and future of color management, alongside common terms. With this background and vocabulary, we're ready for our first stop: Photoshop.

After learning how an image editor handles color, we'll move onto the web and survey its evolving color needs. We'll end with apps, for both mobile and desktop, and see how wider color gamuts can make your work shine.

# PHOTOSHOP

ADOBE HAS BEEN CONCERNED with processing color for a long time—remember when I talked about scanning film and printing with inks? Photoshop (and other desktop publishing apps) needed to manage color as soon as that first pixel came off the scanner on its way to the printer; color management has been part of the editor since version 5.0 for Mac and Windows in 1998.

In this chapter, we'll go deep into the specifics of Photoshop; we'll then take those techniques and close out the chapter with a method you can apply to any other tool.

I've found some people still believe the way to get consistent display of color across development tools is to turn off Photoshop's color management and work directly with the monitor's RGB color profile. While that was once true, the way our apps handle color has changed—for the better. But these improvements aren't universal across platforms, which spells complications.

Apple has recently adopted color management in its desktop apps. Other apps, like web browsers that need to work on platforms outside macOS, don't manage color for all content.

You end up with a situation in which, at this writing, the most recent versions of Safari and Preview support color profiles while Chrome and Firefox don't. As a result, those four apps *can't* display a single color value the same way. Compounding the problem is that *many mobile devices don't manage color*, but many *desktop tools do.*

Given these color disparities, our friend Photoshop needs some attention. Don't worry; you'll create UI graphics as you've always done. But you'll need to set the right levers prior to using "Save for Web" or the new "Export As."

Before we get cranking: this chapter shows screenshots from Photoshop CS6 and CC 2015. Even though Adobe introduced color management many years ago, the terminology and features have not changed much. Some of the controls may look different in your version, but they'll work the same.

# WORKING SPACE

Let's open a sample PSD file, ColorTest.psd.zip. You can experiment with it as we go through our color settings. (If you get a "Missing Profile" dialog, select "Leave as is" and press OK.)

To start, you'll want to know which color profile Photoshop is using. The easiest way to find out is through the menu in the lower-left corner of the main window (marked with a right arrow). Select Document Profile (**FIG 2.1**).

You should see "Untagged RGB," which means the ColorTest. psd file was saved without an embedded profile. Photoshop automatically displays files without profiles using Photoshop's working color space. Let's review that setting now.

## Hello, Color Settings

Under the Edit menu, open Color Settings... (⇧⌘K). Under Working Spaces, check RGB. For this exercise, make sure it's set as "sRGB IEC61966-2.1" (**FIG 2.2**).

(From here on, I'll refer to this color space as *sRGB*. That long stretch of numbers references the International Electrotechnical Commission 1999 standard, which specifies this profile's CIEXYZ values.)

Since we're focusing on how to manage color on computer displays, we can safely ignore CMYK and the other choices. We'll visit Color Management Policies later on.

Let's return to the document. As you hover over each color, the Info palette shows the RGB value that's stored in the file: (255, 0, 0), (102, 0, 204), (123, 45, 67), or (12, 34, 56). Pretty straightforward, right? We'll call those values the "raw" colors. Next, open your computer's Digital Color Meter and make sure it's set to "Display native values" (which, as the name suggests, shows the actual colors displayed on screen). If you're using xScope, select Loupe > Working Color Space > Display RGB.

Hover over the colors again—you'll see the numbers don't line up with Photoshop's values (**FIG 2.3**). On my display, Digital Color Meter reports the colors as (255, 1, 15), (121, 1, 204), (128, 41, 69), and (21, 38, 59). The values on your

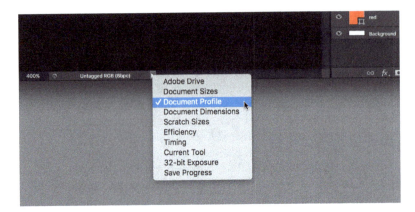

FIG 2.1: Configuring Photoshop to show the current document's color profile.

FIG 2.2: Setting the working space to sRGB.

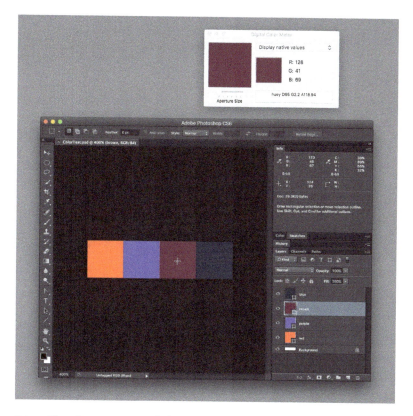

**FIG 2.3:** The colors on screen aren't the same as those in the file.

display will differ from mine. Why are these reported values so different from the raw ones? And why don't they match across displays?

Remember, we started with RGB values, but our file didn't have a color profile. When that happens, Photoshop translates colors into your specified working space before sending them to your display; in this case, it translated the raw color into sRGB.

To see Photoshop's sRGB colors, set the Digital Color Meter or xScope to "Display in sRGB." Think of this option as "app is set to sRGB"—you're giving the tool a hint about an image

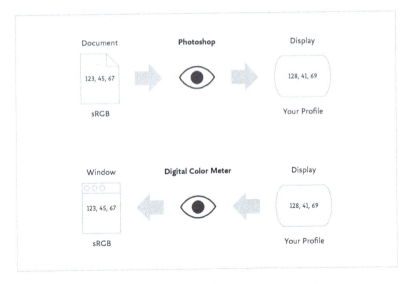

**FIG 2.4:** The Digital Color Meter reverses the display process in Photoshop.

editor's working space, as the tool has no way to ask Photoshop (or any other app) how it's displaying pixels.

With this hint, the Digital Color Meter converts first your display's native values into a device-independent number (based on the color profile for the eye), and then into sRGB. The process is called an *inverse transformation*, because it's the exact opposite of what Photoshop is doing—converting color from sRGB to the eye to the display (**FIG 2.4**).

When Photoshop and the color sampler both use the same color profiles for your display, eye, and file, the numeric values begin to agree (**FIG 2.5**).

Some reported values will still be slightly off, because you lose a bit of information in the color conversion to and from sRGB for display. It's like clipping in an audio signal: when an amplifier tries to push a sound to the point where the system can't handle it, no amount of attenuation can recover the lost signal. In color management, the biggest limiting factor is the gamut of the color space. sRGB represents a small range; in our

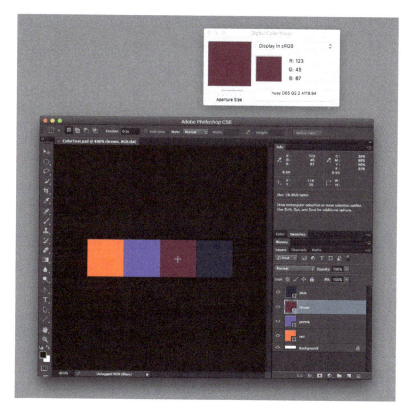

**FIG 2.5:** Photoshop and Digital Color Meter now match, because they're both using sRGB.

example, the red and purple colors shift the most—these highly saturated colors push the boundaries.

## Your working space options

We set Photoshop's color profile to sRGB, but let's see how other profiles look. Go to Edit > *Color Settings...* and check the Preview box. (Have you memorized ⇧⌘K yet? You will have by the end of this book!)

The RGB working space lists:

- Monitor RGB
- Adobe RGB (1998)
- Apple RGB
- ColorMatch RGB
- ProPhoto RGB
- sRGB IEC61966-2.1

And many more. Go ahead and pick a few, to see how the colors change with each setting. You can also adjust the Digital Color Meter to match the raw values, as you did with sRGB.

Now choose Monitor RGB. If you test the native color values with Digital Color Meter, they're the same as the raw values from the file. You might think, *Perfect match!*

Nope.

## Problems with Monitor RGB

The key to this not-so-perfect match lies in the name: the *monitor*.

Your monitor differs from mine. Your monitor might differ from someone else's on your team. Your monitor probably differs from your client's.

And these differences can cause color problems that are hard to figure out.

For example, say you use *Monitor RGB* while editing screenshots; you won't get any color shifts since the images are tagged with your display's color profile when they're captured. But this only works as long as you edit the files on *the same monitor*. When someone sends you a new file, it's unlikely your display is exactly like theirs, and you'll wind up with color shifts.

Even Photoshop has trouble with multiple monitors. If you're lucky enough to have more than one display, you might be surprised to learn Monitor RGB only applies to a single display—the primary one. If you're working on a document on a secondary display, a profile mismatch results, which shifts colors (and trying to pinpoint why could waste hours of your day).

Because of Monitor RGB's inherent unpredictability, I strongly recommend choosing sRGB as your working space. Browsers are starting to use it as a default, and sRGB is often the only color space supported by mobile platforms. As you'll see in a bit, choosing sRGB also minimizes your chance of screwing things up when saving files.

# EMBEDDED PROFILES

We've looked at how Photoshop displays a file without an embedded profile. But you'll probably come across PSD files with profiles—not every designer or developer uses the same Photoshop color settings as you do. (Weird, right?)

When you open a document with an embedded profile, Photoshop detects the profile, and handles it based on your Color Management Policies under Color Settings. Let's explore those settings.

### Default Color Settings

By default, Photoshop sets the RGB working space as sRGB and the color management policy as Preserve Embedded Profiles. The various "Ask When" options are also off. Hit ⇧⌘K and take a moment to make sure your Color Settings match the defaults (FIG 2.6).

Heads up: you might want to take a screenshot of your current settings because we're going to make a lot of changes. Since many of the dialogs that follow have a "Don't show again" option, use Reset All Warning Dialogs in Preferences › General... to make them reappear.

Last, check that you still have Document Profile selected in the lower-left corner of the Photoshop window, as we'll refer to it often.

### Preserving embedded profiles

Let's open a sample file with an embedded sRGB color profile, ColorTest-sRGB.psd. Since we enabled Preserve Embedded Profiles, the document retains its profile: you'll see sRGB in the lower-left corner of the main window. That your working space is also set to sRGB isn't a factor here—a saved profile will override Photoshop's default.

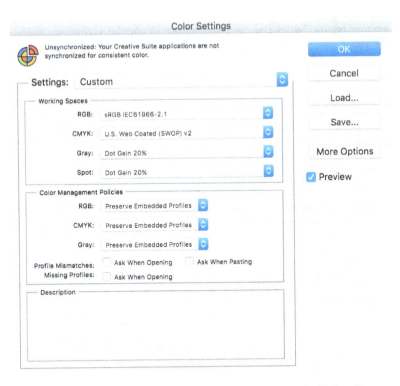

FIG 2.6: Photoshop's default color settings use sRGB and preserve embedded profiles.

To verify this, download another PSD, ColorTest-Generic-RGB.psd. Once you open the file, Photoshop will alert you to a profile mismatch; select "use the embedded profile." You'll see Generic RGB Profile in the lower left—compare how Photoshop renders its pixels to the initial sRGB-embedded file: the generic profile is much lighter than its sRGB counterpart.

(The change in brightness happens because the generic profile, from older versions of macOS, uses a different gamma value from sRGB's. It's also the reason many designers complained about the screen being "too dark" when the Mac switched in 2009.)

Embedding a color profile isn't limited to PSD files: here's a PNG, ColorTest-MonitorRGB.png, with my monitor profile attached. If you open it in Photoshop, you'll see the document profile in its usual place. Or, if you want to skip Photoshop, you can check profiles with the Preview app: go to the Inspector panel (⌘I) and look at the ColorSync profile field. This trick also works with JPEG and PSD files. Some files—most notably GIF—don't allow embedded color profiles as part of their file format specifications.

Take a look at the three files. All three started with the same raw color values—the red is still (255, 0, 0), which you can verify using Photoshop's Info palette—but each file's embedded profile directs how the pixels are transformed on their way to the screen.

Next, let's visit some other options for Color Management Policies. Time for ⇧⌘K.

## Discarding embedded profiles

The color management policy has an Off option. You've likely used this before if you've set Monitor RGB as your working space: Off is the only choice.

The problem with that setting is it throws away important information.

For instance, take ColorTest-GenericRGB.psd. When you open the file and the policy is Off, Photoshop may warn you that the color in the document doesn't match your current working space (FIG 2.7).

As soon as you select OK, Photoshop loses track of the fact that I created the file with a Generic RGB color space. Worse, you may not even realize it—the warning box has an option for "Don't show again," and if you've checked it in the past, you're discarding data by default.

Either way, you end up with "Untagged RGB" as the document profile in the main window, and Photoshop will display the raw color values in the file as sRGB, your current working space.

You've created a situation where our green lights don't agree. My green light used Generic RGB; your green light uses sRGB. On top of that, you threw away the box my green light came in, so you have no way to get back to the color I was looking at.

**Embedded Profile Mismatch**

The document "ColorTest-GenericRGB.psd" has an embedded color profile that does not match the current RGB working space. The current RGB color management policy is to discard profiles that do not match the working space.

Embedded:  Generic RGB Profile

Working:  sRGB IEC61966-2.1

Don't show again          Cancel          OK

**FIG 2.7:** Warning: you're about to lose vital information in your image.

**Embedded Profile Mismatch**

The document "ColorTest-GenericRGB.psd" has an embedded color profile that does not match the current RGB working space. The document's colors will be converted to the working space.

Embedded:  Generic RGB Profile

Working:  sRGB IEC61966-2.1

Don't show again          Cancel          OK

**FIG 2.8:** Photoshop is on the verge of changing every color in your file.

To sum up: don't discard profiles by using Off.

But since your working space is set to sRGB, would it make sense to convert the image? (Trick question!)

## Convert to Working RGB

Let's tackle the last RGB policy option in our trusty Color Settings... Select Convert to Working RGB. Now open ColorTest-GenericRGB.psd, and you might see another profile-mismatch message (**FIG 2.8**).

When you click OK, Photoshop converts the file's raw color values from Generic RGB Profile to sRGB. Sounds good!

Until you realize that all the raw color values in your file just got modified. Your (255, 0, 0) is now (255, 38, 0), (102, 0, 204) is (123, 44, 214), etc. Go ahead and verify this with Photoshop's Info palette.

When you're working with user interface graphics and other assets for development, permanently converting pixels is rarely something you want to do.

Why would Adobe provide such a dangerous feature? Again, it's in the name: *Photo*. You're focused on UI work, but other folks are processing pictures. Unlike you, photographers aren't interested in individual pixel values: they're concerned with how the overall image is perceived. Photoshop's conversion process makes an image with a Generic RGB profile look the same when presented in sRGB—note how the lighter colors remain, even though sRGB has a darker color gamut.

This is exactly what a photographer with a high-end DSLR wants when their picture is in a wider gamut (like Adobe RGB or ProPhoto), and they need a predictable presentation in the web's more limited sRGB. The photo will lose some dynamic range, but perceptually it will still hew closer to the original.

You'll want the same thing—like when you're working on a website hero image that has to match colors in CSS. Converting to an sRGB working space lets you preserve the photo's look and prevent color shifts on different screens.

So wouldn't it be great if you could make a choice for every file you open?

## "Ask When"

The engineers at Adobe have you covered.

The Color Management Policies section has three check-boxes that cause Photoshop to ask what to do when it detects a profile problem. You'll get a dialog box with options to: use the embedded profile, convert document colors to your working space, or discard the embedded profile (FIG 2.9).

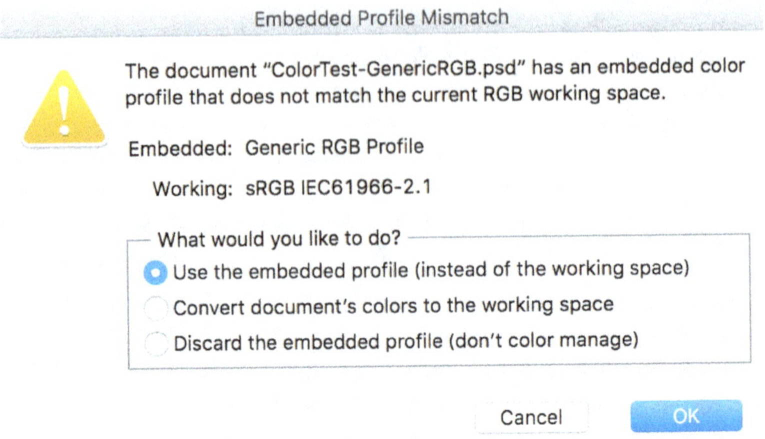

**Embedded Profile Mismatch**

The document "ColorTest-GenericRGB.psd" has an embedded color profile that does not match the current RGB working space.

Embedded: Generic RGB Profile

Working: sRGB IEC61966-2.1

┌─ What would you like to do? ─────────────────────────────┐
- ⦿ Use the embedded profile (instead of the working space)
- ◯ Convert document's colors to the working space
- ◯ Discard the embedded profile (don't color manage)
└──────────────────────────────────────────────────────────┘

Cancel     OK

**FIG 2.9:** Photoshop lets you choose what to do when it detects a file that's not in your working space.

I recommend turning on all of the "Ask When" options for a couple reasons:

- Information in the dialog gives you a better idea of what's happening with each file.
- You can decide case by case how to handle any profile discrepancies.

When the profile-mismatch dialog appears, your choices boil down to:

- "Use the embedded profile" if you want to see what the person who created the file was looking at. Photoshop will adapt the colors to your own display. The color match probably won't be exact, as your display differs from the one where the file originated, but the color will be as close as it can be. This setting is the same as the earlier Preserve Embedded Profile policy—it's likely your safest and best choice.

- "Convert document's colors to the working space" if you're working with a photograph and need it to look right in your sRGB development environment. Don't choose this if you're working with UI graphics. (As you'll see later, altering color values isn't necessary if your target platform can display photos with a profile.)
- "Discard the embedded profile" if you're absolutely sure the person who created the image worked with raw values—and that's all you want from the file. Photoshop will take the raw color values in the file and present them in your working space (which should be set to sRGB). This is the same behavior as when the RGB color management policy is Off. I think of this as expert mode: you're opting to work without a profile at a point when you don't know how color management will affect your results. As we'll learn, it's better to defer this decision until you've opened the file and can see what happens to the image when the profile is removed.

Whatever you choose as the RGB color management policy in Color Settings... will be the default radio button. If you use Preserve Embedded Profile most of the time, all you'll need to do is press Enter in the mismatch dialog.

Finally, have you ever wondered about the octothorp or asterisk that appears after the color space and image depth in Photoshop's window title or tab? Photoshop displays an "#" after "RGB/8" if the current document doesn't have a color profile. When the document profile isn't the same as the working space, you'll see an "*" instead. It's a handy way to remember if you preserved or discarded the original color profile.

## Assigning profiles

Wouldn't it be nice if you could see what your raw color values looked like with different profiles? Or how your document would look if you disabled color management? You can do so with Assign Profile... in Photoshop's Edit menu (**FIG 2.10**).

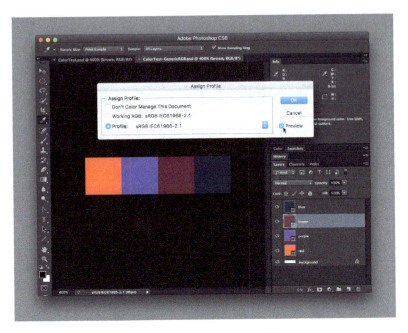

FIG 2.10: Preview color profiles with Photoshop's Assign Profile feature.

When you assign a profile, the raw color values stay the same. You're only specifying how Photoshop should present those values when a profile is selected or removed. Check the box to get a live preview.

Let's open a sample image, **Image-ProPhoto.jpg** (preserve the embedded profile). In the Assign Profile... dialog, you can select any of the current profiles in the dropdown and preview them. If you choose sRGB, you'll get an excellent approximation of how that file will look on a mobile device or in a web browser without color management.

The live preview also demonstrates what happens when you discard the profile, with "Don't Color Manage." (Now you'll know if that's the wisest course, instead of dropping it from the start.)

### Converting profiles

Also under Photoshop's Edit menu, Convert to Profile... *does* modify your document's raw pixels (to preserve the appearance of the file). This option can be useful if you're dealing with photography or other types of images where the color values for individual pixels aren't important—say, if you're focused on the overall range of tones in a photo.

But when you're dealing with UI graphics, converting colors from one profile to another does more harm than good: your carefully crafted RGB values will change. For the most part, steer clear of this feature.

## SAVE FOR WEB: AND EVERYTHING ELSE

So far, we've looked at how Photoshop handles color while you're editing. It's important to understand how to manage colors as you create graphics, but that work will be for naught if you don't correctly save the file.

Despite its name, Save for Web applies to every kind of file in our web and app work; it'd be more apt to call it Save for Everything. And it brings a whole Swiss Army knife set of options—and as you're about to see, while some are a great help, others can cause confusion or errors in your development workflow. (The color shift in Dr. Eyeful's logo occurred because one checkbox in Save for Web was incorrectly set.)

Let's run through the settings for saving our work.

### Keep an eyedropper on things

One of my favorite features of the Save for Web window is the eyedropper.

Hover over any color in the graphic, and see the raw RGB value displayed below the output preview. It's a great way to make a last-minute check that the colors in your user interface are right.

Click on any color, and Photoshop will save it in the well on the left. Clicking the color well will convert the color to a web hex value or any of the other formats supported by Photoshop. You can also add the color to your swatches for later reference.

### sRGB color conversion

By default, Photoshop has the Convert to sRGB checkbox ticked.

Like Convert to Profile, Convert to sRGB changes the raw color values in your file. When you leave it on, if your document has a color profile, your colors may be mangled on save, and you'll end up with a file in production that doesn't match your source Photoshop document. (And you wonder why designers and developers fight!)

Of course, if you're working in the sRGB color space, you won't see a difference whether the feature is on or off, since there's nothing to convert. Still, for those times you're not in sRGB—however rare—it's better to be safe than to risk losing profile information.

Turn Convert to sRGB off, and leave it that way (FIG 2.11).

(If you really need to convert pixel color values from one space to another, stick with Convert to Profile. You'll have more control over the process, and it'll be easier to compare the image before and after.)

### Embedding profiles

Above all else, you need to understand the Embed Color Profile checkbox. When it's checked, the current profile you're using for editing will be added to the file. No color values are changed; the profile tells other software how to process the data for display.

This sounds good on the surface. But remember, there's little consistency to how apps manage color. Safari handles colors differently from Chrome. The same goes for color management on a mobile device (with limited resources) versus a desktop computer.

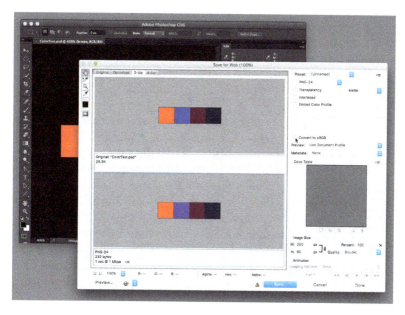

FIG 2.11: Saving the image without sRGB conversion or an embedded profile.

So when should you embed a profile? Two rules can help:

- If the file is a photograph for a web page or an app, *embed a profile*. The profile gives the system a chance to render an image closer to what you were editing in Photoshop.
- If the file is an image for a user interface, *do not embed a profile*. (We'll examine why when we look at platforms in upcoming chapters. The web browsers in Chapter 3 are full of surprises!)

If you don't embed a profile, you'll also reduce the file size by a couple thousand bytes (the Save for Web preview shows you the exact figure). This is inconsequential for a large photo, but for interface graphics, which tend to multiply like rabbits, these kilobytes can add up to a lot of space.

If you do embed a profile, make sure it makes sense for both the source image and the viewing environment. Here are some guidelines, based on common profiles:

- **sRGB** looks good on a variety of devices, but as the lowest common denominator, it seldom looks awesome. Embedding this profile is also redundant: it's the default when one isn't present in the file. Worse, embedding sRGB in graphics can cause a mismatch with the same color in CSS.
- **Adobe RGB** is ideal when you're working with digital photos, as many cameras capture images in this color space. As with ColorMatch RGB and ProPhoto RGB, this profile can display a wider range of colors (all three have a larger gamut than sRGB). They also produce more vibrant, accurate colors when the images are printed. On the downside, the superior color is lost on many mobile devices.
- **Generic RGB** looks fine on a Mac but feels washed out on a PC. (It's a good idea to do cross-platform testing when embedding profiles.)
- Never embed your **Monitor RGB** profile, unless you plan on shipping your display to everyone who visits your website.

Whether you embed or not, keep the setting consistent on a given type of image or project (e.g., make sure a website's hero images embed the same profile). Use the Inspector panel in Preview to double-check a file's embedded profile. If a profile exists, you'll see it listed as ColorSync profile. If the field is blank, Photoshop (or another app) saved the image without an embedded profile.

For an in-depth discussion on how to get the most out of your digital photos, check out Color Space and Color Profiles from the American Society of Media Photographers. "AdobeRGB vs. sRGB" from Fstoppers lays out the differences between the two profiles.

# EXPORT AS: A NEW KID ON THE BLOCK

We've saved the best for last. (Working for Dr. Eyeful has taken its toll in the wordplay department.)

Save for Web was introduced in Photoshop 5.5 in 1999. Sixteen years later, a new way to save graphics arrived in Photoshop CC: Export As.

Why does Photoshop need another way to save images? We've just seen that Save for Web is a perfectly capable tool for outputting files and managing color.

We've also seen a user interface that has a lot of levers, which can be daunting when all you need to do is save a part of your document. And behind that complex interface is code originally written in 1998 for a web that only supported GIF and JPEG images. Many of our needs have changed since those days, but our tools and workflows haven't. The engineers at Adobe are using the new Export As to make a clear break from the past, to give everyone a chance to work more efficiently.

The venerable Save for Web isn't going away—it's still there (for now, and we'll see why in a minute), but it's labeled Legacy and won't get any further love from its developers.

## Better? You bet!

Change is hard, and we resist it unless something is in it for us. Luckily, we have a lot to like about the new Export As dialog:

- The biggest improvement is you can now export multiple layers and artboards at once. Anyone who's ever cut up the layers of a Photoshop document to create files for an app or website has known the pain of pressing the ⌥⇧⌘S key combination over and over and over. With Export As, you can select items and save them as a batch. If you have a lot of layers, this saves a ton of time.
- Assets can be scaled as they're saved—letting you quickly create normal and higher-resolution graphics (commonly referred to as @1x, @2x and @3x assets).

**FIG 2.12:** The Export As dialog introduced in Photoshop CC 2015.

- Export As supports SVG files. As designs have simplified in recent years, the use of shapes in layers has increased. Saving these types of images in a vector format often decreases their size considerably. As you'd expect, the Export As dialog shows how many bytes each format will use.

The best part is it's all done in a user interface that's much simpler than what we've seen with Save for Web (**FIG 2.12**).

Diving into the specifics of Export As is beyond this book's scope, but Adobe has plenty of terrific documentation to get you up to speed—start with the video tutorial.

### But not quite yet

Given these great features, why is Adobe keeping Save for Web?

Writing good software takes time, and Export As is clearly a work in progress. Adobe has been straightforward about missing functionality, and has promised to bring features from Save for Web to this new interface. For example, the initial release of CC in 2015 didn't support scaling all assets, converting between color spaces, or including metadata; it added those features five months later in a .1 release.

For now, as of this writing (late 2016), the key deficiencies to consider are:

- Any preview is presented in the screen's color profile—which makes the preview accurate only for images meant for Chrome or Firefox. As a majority of devices and apps use sRGB, you may see some color shifts.
- Export As has no tools to check your work before saving. Save for Web's eyedropper is a handy way to ensure your raw colors are right; likewise, a 2-Up preview lets you look for color changes. Both of these are currently missing.
- If your source document has a color profile assigned, that information is stripped on export. This is fine if you're working with interface graphics, but if you have a hero image or product photo with a wider gamut (such as Adobe RGB or ProPhoto from a high-end DSLR), the lost information will lead to more muted colors.
- If you've used a Timeline to animate your layers, Export As can't save the result as a GIF. It only saves a single frame.

If these features are important to your work, I suggest sticking with Save for Web until the functionality is brought over.

## Convert times two

An unfortunate inclusion in the new export tool is the dreaded Convert to sRGB. Like its predecessor, it's enabled by default and can potentially ruin your work when you save a file.

As before, you need to explicitly turn it off. But Photoshop makes it twice as hard, since the checkbox appears in both

Export As and the Export Preferences panel. In the dialog, each item you're exporting has its own checkbox, and Photoshop keeps track of its state. If you've left the default setting on in the past, you'll need to hunt down each item and turn it off manually. Any new items will get a setting based on the last export. It's convoluted—and another good reason to turn this feature off for good.

The options in Expert Preferences apply when you do a Quick Export—saving files without prompting for settings. If you leave Convert to sRGB on, Photoshop will convert your file on every save.

Instead of removing a dangerous feature, Adobe has made it trickier to permanently disable. Here's hoping they simplify or remove Convert to sRGB in a future release!

## WINDING DOWN WITH SETUP

To recap this chapter on Photoshop's color management:

- Set Color Settings to use a Working Space of sRGB IEC61966-2.1.
- Set RGB Color Management Policies to Preserve Embedded Profiles, with all of the Ask When options turned on.
- Turn off Convert to sRGB when saving images.
- Turn off Embed Color Profile (unless you're saving a photo instead of a UI graphic).

As our industry evolves, you may need to deviate from these recommended settings. For instance, a Display P3 working space may make more sense as displays get deeper. Or you'll need to adapt as Photoshop revisits how it exports files.

The crucial thing is you have the knowledge to make the right decisions and adjust your workflows as necessary—I hope you're now comfortable in the parts of the app that used to make you nervous. (I know I am!)

# OTHER TOOLS

Photoshop isn't the only image editor in town. Many folks prefer other products in place of, or in addition to, this well-known manipulator of pixels; popular alternatives Pixelmator and Acorn, for example, have excellent color-management support.

Much of our work begins with vectors. Whether it's a simple wireframe or a complex illustration, many visual elements start as shapes in an editor. If you're using Illustrator, you'll have the same color-management controls you've seen in Photoshop, and can sync them via Adobe's cloud. Other drawing tools (like Sketch) output images using the sRGB standard.

The tools we use to craft our web pages also have color management built into their editing and previewing functions. Typically, these tools use the same underlying technologies as our browsers. For example, Macaw uses Google's Blink rendering engine, while Coda uses Apple's WebKit. (We'll explore browsers in Chapter 3.)

Last, it's worth noting that most tools on the Mac will use WebKit to render content. (Apple supplies tools for developers to make it easy to include these capabilities.) When in doubt, it's usually safe to assume your tool will display HTML and CSS as Safari does.

For details on how these apps manage color, I've created a web page with the latest information.

## Figure it out

Earlier in this chapter, you used the Digital Color Meter to see how Photoshop displays color. If you encounter an unfamiliar tool and need to know how it manages color, try these simple steps.

Start by creating an area of color with known RGB values, like those we've used throughout this book: (123, 45, 57) for brown or (12, 34, 56) for a dark blue. Then measure what you see on screen with your color meter. If the correct numbers appear when your display is set to sRGB, you'll know the app is using that profile to render your content. Or try different settings to find the closest match.

After you save a file, examine it with the Preview app: the ColorSync profile in the Inspector panel will show you any embedded color information. A dash in this field means no color profile was embedded and sRGB is being used instead. (Remember, this is a good setting for saving web graphics.)

As a final check, make sure the color values you expect are in the previewed file. Set your color meter to the same profile shown in the Preview Inspector, and verify the values match.

# WEB BROWSERS

WHILE PHOTOSHOP is a formidable tool for managing the color of your graphics, it's only half of the equation: another app will present your artwork. It's nearly impossible to create an image without thinking about how it will be parsed by HTML and CSS; even native apps use the web in creative ways (including showcasing products in Apple's App Store).

When we talk about color on the web, we're talking about browsers—they turn markup like #ff0000 into a red that people see on the page, and they process our images and any embedded color profiles.

(To be clear, we aren't talking about the rendering framework that puts elements on the page. Something like WebKit isn't responsible for processing color, and as you'll see, framework behavior varies wildly depending on where it's used.)

Commercial browsers—which surfaced in the early 1990s—predate the color-management systems we use now. As such, the web began with a pretty simple view on color. For instance, the #00 to #ff hex representation is a way to specify the 0-255 range we've used throughout this book. But when you drop #00ff00 into your code, there's no mention of a color profile. Will that green hex value match my light bulb? Or yours?

Or take web images, which can have embedded profiles. How will browsers handle those? How can you predict what color your visitor will land on?

To answer these questions, let's start with some guidance from the World Wide Web Consortium (W3C).

## SRGB, MAYBE

Here's what the web standards body has to say about color values:

*All RGB colors are specified in the sRGB color space.*

It's our friend sRGB! But pay careful attention—the W3C says "specified," which doesn't necessarily cover how colors are *presented*:

*User agents may vary in the fidelity with which they represent these colors, but using sRGB provides an unambiguous and objectively measurable definition of what the color should be, which can be related to international standards.*

When the W3C says that user agents "may vary the fidelity," they're letting browser makers bend the rules. When we use colors in CSS stylesheets and image elements, everyone agrees they're sRGB. When those same colors are displayed on a *web page*, results vary, depending on what you're trying to draw. Let's explore the forms that color can take in your browser.

## Good old images

Images have been an integral part of the web from its inception. Since the late '90s, browsers have treated raster graphics without embedded profiles as sRGB—a de facto standard established before the official W3C spec.

In 2005, Safari 2.0 was the first browser to support images with embedded profiles. Safari did something similar to what you saw in Photoshop: it transformed the pixels from the embedded color profile to the screen's color space. After seven years, all desktop browsers had the same capability.

This sounds great until you realize we're talking just the desktop. We'll see very different behavior from mobile browsers in a bit.

## Exciting new graphics

*Scalable vector graphics* (SVG) are increasingly common assets in our web interfaces. According to the W3C specification for SVG 1.1, all colors default to the sRGB color space and use the same formatting as CSS2. Yay!

But then:

*Additionally, SVG content can specify an alternate color specification using an ICC profile as described in Specifying paint. If ICC-based colors are provided and the SVG user agent supports*

*ICC color, then the ICC-based color takes precedence over the sRGB color specification...*

Currently, no user agents support these embedded color profiles, but it's clear the standards folks see SVG as a color-managed vector file format, with the same stature as JPEG and PNG for raster images. Don't assume SVG will always be sRGB.

### Drawing on the canvas

The specification for the canvas element states that drawing should use the same color management as img elements and CSS. In practice, that means canvas correctly handles embedded profiles and anything you draw into the 2D context will render in sRGB. A test page, Canvas Test, shows several examples of how color varies with a canvas element.

As other elements on the page adapt to color management, canvas likely will as well. At this writing, members of the WHATWG are discussing adding a color space parameter when you create a context.

### Evolving CSS color

You're still most likely to specify a color via CSS. Yet as you saw, the W3C isn't strict on how that color appears on the page. Since browser-makers have their own goals, developers now face a situation where Apple and Google interpret the standard differently.

This is not the first time browser-makers have disagreed on what is best! Let's check out the nuances to this discord—and potential headaches in our workflow.

## BROWSER COLOR ENTANGLEMENT

A picture's worth a thousand words, so let's open a test page in both Safari and Chrome on macOS (**FIG 3.1**).

The images on the page come from the **ColorTest.psd** file in Chapter 2. The groups of color on the right are PNG images

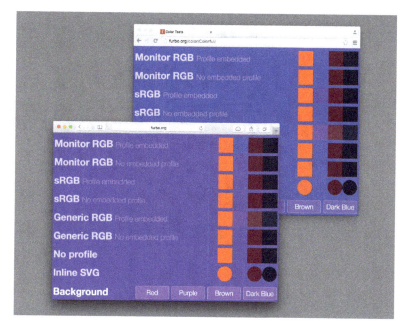

FIG 3.1: The same page, two browsers: Safari (front) and Chrome (back) on macOS.

(the square sets) and inline SVG (the round set). The background colors are generated with CSS.

Each image file was created from the Photoshop document with assigned Monitor RGB, sRGB, and Generic RGB profiles. Two images were saved with each profile: one with and one without Embed Color Profile. The background CSS colors use the same values entered in Photoshop.

You may not see as pronounced a difference between the two browsers; the exact results depend on your computer's display.

When you open the page on a mobile device, the colors in the images change depending on your operating system (FIG 3.2).

All browsers share the same markup, yet colors vary in both the CSS and images (some slight, some more obvious). This is a big deal—let's zoom in.

FIG 3.2: The test page in Safari on iOS (left) and Android (right).

# MANAGING COLORS IN CSS

In FIG 3.1, you'll notice that the background colors on the pages aren't quite the same. The reason is simple: Safari and Chrome use different display color spaces to render CSS. Apple started diverging years ago with the 10.9 Mavericks release, and continued more recently with the iOS 9.3 release. The changes, sparked by better display technology, have been a long time coming—we'll probably see more as computer hardware improves.

Let's take a look at why color management differs across browsers and how it affects your development environment.

### Safari pushes forward

Apple found itself in a tough situation: it wanted to improve displays *and* support standard web colors. The WebKit developers have wanted to make their browser "color smart" for years but were stymied by Flash. The decline of that technology and the introduction of new DCI-P3 displays gave developers an opportunity to use color management and have the best of both worlds.

Now, when you specify a color in CSS, Safari takes the raw color values and puts them in an sRGB color space. That color is then transformed using color management to the display's profile. If you type #6600cc in your CSS, it produces something like #7900cf on screen.

You can check for yourself: on our Colorful test page, compare the sRGB (Profile embedded) sample against the background colors. Since the image and CSS colors match, they must use the same profile. Note also images *without* profiles match the sRGB image: Safari uses the same default color space for both types of content.

Safari's new behavior means you need to make sure your tools can take a display color space and convert it back to sRGB—otherwise, you'll sample #7900cf on screen and wonder why it doesn't appear in your code. (Both Digital Color Meter and xScope do this conversion, so you're set.)

You'll also need to pay attention when using Photoshop's eyedropper, which samples color using the display's color profile. When you specify a CSS color as (255, 0, 0) and then grab it from a page in Safari, you'll end up with something like (250, 20, 27) in Photoshop's color well. You won't see this color shift when you sample the same page in Chrome. (I'll explain why in the next section.)

Apple isn't out to make everyone's life more difficult with these changes: again, it wants to give us better displays and follow web standards. Think of Safari's sRGB as a compatibility mode for a DCI-P3 screen that has a lot more color than its peers.

## Colors everywhere else

All other browsers, including Chrome, don't touch your CSS colors. Anything you specify in your code goes directly to the screen and adopts its color profile. See this in play in FIG 3.1 by comparing the CSS background and the embedded profiles: the color *does* match my Mac's Monitor RGB and *does not* match sRGB.

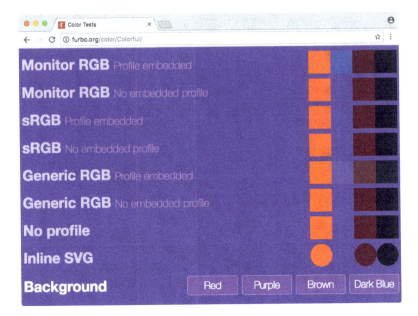

FIG 3.3: The test page on a Thunderbolt Display.

Don't forget: unless you have my Dell monitor and the calibration tool I used to create the profile, you won't see that perfect match when *you* view Monitor RGB. Instead you might see something similar to what Apple's Thunderbolt Display produces (FIG 3.3).

Now Monitor RGB looks completely wrong and sRGB is close but still a little off. Here are a couple lessons about these color shifts:

- Never embed your display's color profile in an image. Everyone but you will see the wrong color.
- Many displays have gamuts that are very close to the sRGB standard, but not exact. If you embed the sRGB profile in a graphic, you're at the browser's mercy when it comes to

matching the colors. While it's obvious in FIG 3.1, it's subtle enough in FIG 3.3 to drive a perfectionist up a wall.

Chrome's use of the display's color space may seem a bit counterintuitive, especially when the W3C recommends using sRGB. But if you assume most displays will be close to this color space, no color compensation is required. For a product that must work on different platforms and devices—many of which don't support color management—this is a pragmatic engineering decision. Firefox does the same thing, for the same reason.

You can use this behavior to your advantage during development. If you want to check CSS colors from the display with no color space conversions, use Chrome, Firefox, or Internet Explorer to display the page. Tools like Photoshop's eyedropper will pick the exact color that was in your code.

## Working with Windows

Many folks will still view your work on Windows, especially if you're targeting things like corporate intranets—you may even use this OS as your primary development platform.

Though it only needs to support a personal computer, the last version of Internet Explorer displays color much like what we've seen with Chrome (FIG 3.4).

But you'll see one small difference: the sRGB image matches the background exactly, because Windows uses sRGB as a system-wide default. Until recently, if you wanted to run an app in another color space, you needed to install extra software. But Windows 10 lets you calibrate a display and replace its profile.

You can configure your Mac to behave like Windows, which is helpful if you're working on a site that will net lots of visits from a PC. Open System Preferences > Displays, and in the Color panel, select "sRGB IEC61966-2.1." After you relaunch your browsers, they'll mimic what would happen on Windows; as a bonus, all your browsers will use the same colors when rendering CSS. You might miss the beauty of your Mac's built-in color profile, but you'll have a better idea of what others are seeing.

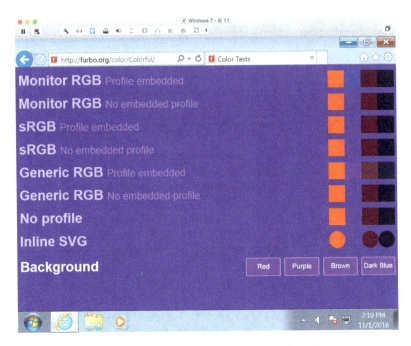

FIG 3.4: The test page running in Internet Explorer 11 on a virtual machine: yet another variation.

## CSS changes ahead

To sum up, Safari is the oddball in rendering CSS colors. But we could've said the same in 2005 when Safari was the only browser to correctly render embedded color profiles. Seven years later, all browsers did. As display hardware continues to improve, other browser makers will likely follow the WebKit team's lead. Time will tell.

It's clear the W3C wants to improve color management on the web. The days of sRGB as the lone color space for CSS may be numbered: the original proposal for the CSS3 color module included a color-profile property. Although it was dropped in the current implementations, the standards folks would still like to see it in the future. If and when this happens, CSS will be able to embed profiles, just like images.

Further, another proposal suggests adding a new `color()` function that extends the familiar `rgb()` with a color space name. To get a fully saturated red in DCI-P3, you'd be able to specify something like `color(p3 1.0 0.0 0.0)` instead of `rgb(100%, 0%, 0%)`.

# MOBILE COLOR ADVANCES

While browsers on a PC or your laptop all render images as expected, results when you're away from the desk are mixed.

The capabilities of early mobile devices were meager. Processing an image eats a lot of power and memory, and photos—the assets most likely to have color profiles—can have millions of pixels. But in recent years, the devices we carry in our pockets and bags have become a lot more powerful, sometimes even more capable than what we have on our desktops. As a result, color management on mobile is catching up.

### Color in your pocket

It might surprise you to learn that Microsoft's new Edge browser (Project Spartan) for Windows 10 was the first mobile browser to correctly handle embedded color profiles (**FIG 3.5**). But it makes sense: since Windows 10 is a unified system that works on both mobile and desktop, consistent handling of color between the two is crucial. As a company, Microsoft also has a long history of maintaining backward compatibility—compare the screenshot of IE 11 in **FIG 3.4** with Edge's in **FIG 3.5**.

Like Microsoft, Apple is a company with a browser that works on both platforms. But Apple has another factor that makes color management essential: it's beginning to produce better displays for both desktop (iMac) and mobile (iPad Pro). The new DCI-P3 display standard has "a color standard big enough for Hollywood."

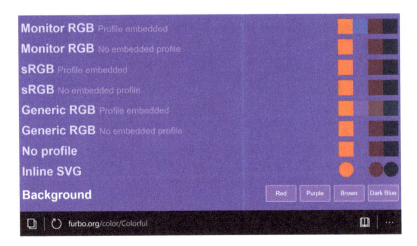

FIG 3.5: Microsoft's latest browser showing the test page on Windows 10 Mobile.

DCI-P3 gives the iPad Pro 25% greater color saturation. To display sRGB (which has a narrower color gamut) on this device, the WebKit developers needed color management. So they brought Safari's desktop capabilities to mobile in the iOS 9.3 release. In Figs **3.1** and **3.2**, you'll see the browser render the CSS and image content identically.

Be aware that Safari's ability to use color profiles depends on the device's age; older phones and tablets don't have the processing power to convert colors, and that can lead to surprising shifts (**FIG 3.6**). The first chip to boast this new capability was the A8, which first appeared in the iPhone 6.

The last key piece of the mobile ecosystem is Android. The sad news is this platform doesn't support color management. In **FIG 3.2**, you'll see all images render the same, whether or not they have an embedded profile. You'll also get the left-hand results of **FIG 3.6**, even on the latest devices.

It's always difficult to predict the future, but given the intense competition in the mobile industry, it's easy to imagine that Samsung and other manufacturers will want their displays to top Apple's. They'll need color management to keep up.

**FIG 3.6:** A wide-gamut image displayed on an older mobile device (left) and a newer one (right). Photograph by Jeff Carlson.

## Responsive color

From the survey of mobile browsers, you know only some of your visitors will have color management. As a conscientious developer, you stick with sRGB. But wide-gamut images on a P3 screen (like on the iPhone 7) are a real marvel—rich and vibrant—and you'd like to offer better color to those who *can* see it.

You're in luck. Picking the right display gamut is just a variation on choosing an image based on screen size and density (@2x). The CSS Working Group has started to tackle this problem with a draft proposal that features a new media query: color-gamut. The media queries you use to check a browser's width and resolution are getting an upgrade for color management.

With the proposed query, your CSS could tailor a hero image on your site to a device's gamut as well as its resolution:

```css
h1#hero {
  background-image: url(hero.jpg);
}
@media (min-resolution: 2dppx) {
  h1#hero {
    background-image: url(hero@2x.jpg);
  }
}
@media (min-resolution: 2dppx) and (color-gamut: p3) {
  h1#hero {
    background-image: url(hero-p3@2x.jpg);
  }
}
```

Don't embed profiles in hero.jpg and hero@2x.jpg, and they'll display correctly as sRGB. With hero-p3@2x.jpg, you can embed a profile with a wider gamut to take advantage of the DCI-P3 display.

If you're dealing with a product catalog or photo gallery, you'll want to do something similar using inline media. Since the venerable img tag doesn't support media queries, use the new hotness, picture:

```html
<picture>
  <source media="(min-resolution: 2dppx) and
    (color-gamut: p3)"
    srcset="photo-p3@2x.jpg">
  <source media="(min-resolution: 2dppx)"
    srcset="photo@2x.jpg">
  <img src="photo.jpg" srcset="photo@2x.jpg 2x"
    alt="A photo">
</picture>
```

Each of the source elements provides a set of images for the browser to use. The media attribute lets the browser load the image that best matches the current display environment. On a high-resolution screen, photo-p3@2x.jpg will load if the device has a wide gamut; otherwise it would display photo@2x.jpg. If the browser doesn't support the picture element or can't find a source match, the img element acts as a fallback. In our example, that's the low-resolution photo.jpg.

Finally, you can incorporate the color-gamut media query into your JavaScript:

```
if (window.matchMedia('(color-gamut: p3)').matches)
  {
  // do something with the wider gamut
  }
```

If you're loading image resources dynamically, you can use the results of this test to adjust your server requests.

To see these techniques in action, take a quick visit to furbo.org/color/ResponsiveColor/. Viewing the source on that page will help you understand what's going on. Note that Safari 10 supports the new color-gamut media query on both iOS and macOS.

Responsive color gives you a way to future-proof your website: as mobile devices gain the power of their desktop counterparts, consistent color across platforms is possible. While you don't know when other browsers will catch up with Safari, you do know they'll follow web standards.

## CONSISTENCY

In the meantime, with these different behaviors among browsers, achieving color consistency may seem a painful enterprise. Happily, it isn't if you follow one rule: *don't embed color profiles if you want your images to match your CSS colors.* This rule applies to most image files when you're building a website: leave out profiles for controls, widgets, and logos.

It's that simple: take another look at the test page in the browser screenshots. When we don't have a color profile, the CSS color and the image color match perfectly in every case. All modern browsers behave the same way. In fact, we should have omitted the color profile from the banner in Dr. Eyeful's site.

The corollary rule is: *embed color profiles in photos selected by a media query.* The query gives you the ability to pick the right image for display and provide backward compatibility.

Remember, there's no point in embedding a profile in a photo that'll use the default sRGB color space. And as we saw in some browsers earlier, embedding a color profile in an image can lead to mismatches with the CSS colors.

It takes extra work to create images with multiple color spaces, as it does to work with graphics in multiple resolutions. So when is it appropriate to make the effort? My guideline is to ask, *Am I selling something?*

Things like hero images that introduce your service to a potential client will look a lot better in a wider gamut. The same goes for photography that makes products appealing. You don't need it for your vacation photos. (To get an idea of how photography improves on a deeper display, I've compiled samples that let you compare sRGB with the wider color spaces of ProPhoto and AdobeRGB.)

One last factor to consider: image optimization. If you use a tool like ImageOptim to make your images mobile-friendly, be aware that these tools often make files smaller by removing color profiles. For example, see the "No profile" row on the Colorful test page. For images meant for a user interface, that's fine. But if you have embedded profiles in your photos, they'll be damaged.

# MOBILE APPS

BECAUSE MANY MOBILE APPS begin their lives as websites, chances are good your web colors will someday become app colors.

The same limitations with memory and processing speeds that exist on the mobile web extend to native apps. Support for color management is limited, and the frameworks to build apps often rely on the display set to sRGB.

Android's specification forgoes color spaces or profiles—colors are specified in the old-school way with three bytes of red, green, and blue. You have to hope each individual manufacturer will present those bytes in something close to sRGB.

Apple, on the other hand, is shaking things up. In iOS 9, Apple added ColorSync support to Core Image, the code that lets you efficiently process graphics. The 9.3 release extended color management to user interfaces in the UIKit framework: UIImageView supported embedded color profiles, and UIColor included CGColorSpace for its RGB properties. iOS 10 continues these advances, with system-wide support for what Apple calls "wide color": you're now able to use profiles with an extended color range and process images with sixteen bits per channel.

The best way to get up to speed on these changes is to watch the videos from WWDC. Color management in iOS is first discussed in WWDC 2015's "What's New In Core Image [Session 510]," starting at 8:50 in the video. Slides 26 and 27 show excellent examples of how color management can improve the display of photography. From 2016, "Working with Wide Color [Session 712]" gives a brief overview of iOS 10's new color capabilities, the ways your development tools and workflows will change, and guidelines for better color in apps. Last, if your app features photographs, be aware the camera we carry in our pockets  can now capture more vibrant imagery: see "Advances in iOS Photography [Session 501]" at the 44-minute mark to learn more.

Phew. Things are in flux, but the engineers at Apple are clearly working toward better color-management support in their OS. It's important to remember that these features are only available on devices with enough processing power—you'll need to consider backward compatibility with older devices.

When you're building an app, you'll face color management at every step of development. To help you understand the considerations involved, let's go through the process with a sample app for iOS 10. Download a ZIP file of the ColorfulMobile project to follow along (you'll need Xcode 8 or later to run it); you'll also see screenshots of the project in this chapter. Comments in the project's code explain options for handling color and resolving problems.

# XCODE

The first step for any iOS app is to open Xcode. Since we've learned that sRGB is common on mobile devices, you might assume sRGB makes sense for your development environment too.

One can only dream. You'll be confronted with different color spaces as you work on your app. Even though iOS defaults to sRGB, storyboards sometimes use a generic color space, while the simulator mirrors your display's color profile. To get consistent color, you'll need to understand these distinctions.

If you haven't already, open the sample project and use the left-hand, dropdown navigation to locate the Main.storyboard file. We'll start the development tour with a common task in customizing a user interface: picking colors.

### Picking colors

In View Controller Scene (the middle panel), click on the brown color bar labeled "123, 45, 67." On the right, select the Attributes inspector panel and click on Background; Xcode's color picker will pop up—make sure you're set to RGB Sliders. If you click on the gear icon, you'll see the color space associated with the chosen color (FIG 4.1). In our screenshot, the brown bar uses the default, sRGB. Use this dropdown menu to set color profiles for the elements in your design, and they'll appear correctly on any device that supports color management. (You can confirm this by firing up the Digital Color Meter.)

**FIG 4.1:** Xcode's color picker sets the color (123, 45, 67) to the sRGB color space.

I built multiple apps in Xcode before I found this profile menu via the gear icon. In older versions, Xcode's default profile was Generic RGB—but most people didn't notice since iOS displayed all colors in sRGB. Here are some other Xcode tips and idiosyncrasies:

- What does this mean for projects from earlier versions of Xcode? When you open one of those storyboards with Xcode 8, it'll automatically convert colors from Generic RGB to sRGB. If you've set your colors to a different profile, Xcode will botch the conversion—because you've given it data it doesn't expect. If you see any color shifts, check both the values and selected profile.

- When you create a new control on your interface, the color space sometimes defaults to Generic RGB instead of sRGB. While this is likely a software bug, double-check via the gear icon before entering RGB values into the text fields.
- Along with the text fields for RGB values or hex codes, Xcode's picker lets you choose colors via eyedropper, crayons, or color wheel. Since these options are shared with other macOS apps, they work with the system's default color space, Generic RGB. Check, and convert to sRGB if needed.
- After you save your storyboard with Xcode 8, your version-control system will note several `colorspace="calibratedRGB"` modifications, as Xcode migrates your colors to `customColorSpace="sRGB"`. Once these changes go through, you won't be able to open the storyboard with an earlier version of Xcode. Make sure everyone on your team is ready to move to iOS 10.

Although you have a choice of color space, I recommend you still use sRGB with Xcode 8. Because the design tool doesn't let you specify more than one profile, working within the narrower gamut will provide the best compatibility across devices. Later in this chapter, you'll learn how to adapt your interface to wider color displays at runtime.

## Compiling image assets

Like your code, an app's image assets are compiled—to optimize them for quick display on a mobile device. To support color management, Xcode brings a new twist to this build phase: wide color. Just as you adapted your design workflow for images with multiple resolutions, you'll now need to think about creating additional resources with new color specifications.

These new assets are wider in memory (with a depth of sixteen bits per channel instead of eight bits) and embed a wider color gamut (using the Display P3 profile). Good thing you got familiar with Photoshop's Color Settings in Chapter 2—you're about to put that knowledge to use!

**FIG 4.2:** The Harbor_Adaptive asset uses both sRGB and Display P3 color spaces.

In the sample project, select the Images.xcassets folder, and the asset catalog will show all the graphics used in the app (for example, AppIcon, ColorTest-Adaptive, Harbor_Adaptive). The catalog has always let you specify images for different types of layouts and devices, and with iOS's new features, color gamut is now an option. Configure the gamut by opening the Attributes inspector (click the slider icon at top right), and choosing "sRGB and Display P3." Pick an image from the catalog, and you'll see outlines of extra assets that need to be filled (**FIG 4.2**).

So what goes in these image cells? Let's look!

### Creating wider assets

The asset catalog supports two bitmap formats: PNG and JPEG. PNG offers lossless compression, which makes sense for smaller files, like controls and other interface elements. Photos and other larger images typically rely on compressed JPEGs that eat up less memory on a mobile device.

Our goal is an image that follows Apple's recommended settings for wide color, which will generate imagery with a higher dynamic range and smoother gradients. So let's loop back to Photoshop, and ready your levers for creating a new PSD document or converting an existing one.

When you're building assets from scratch, the only adjustment is in the New document dialog: set the Color Mode to "16 bit" and the Color Profile (under Advanced) to "Display P3," and you're done!

Sometimes, you'll need to convert assets from third parties, like a photographer or a stock service. These files are often in the JPEG format, which only supports eight bits per channel. To prep these for wide color, first open the file, go to Image > Mode, and set the depth to "16 Bit/Channel." (You can skip this step if you received a TIFF or RAW file saved with 16-bit color.)

(A note on terminology: the number of bits in an image has traditionally indicated its depth. Deeper images have more discrete values in memory, but Apple's documentation focuses on these extra bits working in conjunction with a profile to provide a wider range of color. In this context, deep and wide mean the same thing.)

Once you've adjusted the depth, consider the color space. As noted in Chapter 2, photographers often work in wider gamuts like Adobe RGB or ProPhoto. To retain as much of the original color as possible, use Convert to Profile... with a Destination Space of "Display P3."

Apple recommends saving an asset image as a 16-bit PNG, but, unfortunately, you won't be able to do so with Save for Web or Export As. (Yet. Adobe hasn't updated Photoshop's export features for wide color.) Instead, you'll need to return to Save As... to save the image as a PNG for your asset catalog. If you choose to save an 8-bit JPEG to get a smaller asset, just remember to embed a Display P3 color profile.

These techniques created the 16-bit PNG file for the Harbor_ Adaptive asset in Xcode. (I made the 8-bit version with methods we all know by heart.) Since you'll deal with two files that look very similar, a handy way to verify an asset is to control-click on the cell (for example, "2x Display P3" for Harbor_Adaptive) and select Show in Finder. You'll see Harbor_DisplayP3_16bit.

png, and when you open the file in Preview and view the Inspector, you can check both the depth ("8" or "16") and the profile ("sRGB" or "Display P3").

Before you load your new 16-bit, Display P3 PNG file in Xcode, let's cover how the asset catalog handles an image, and weigh your options.

## Converting colors automatically

Another difference between your UI graphics (PNG) and photos (JPEG) is color conversion. Xcode automatically converts PNG files to the color space a device needs; this conversion can be both a drawback (resulting in unpredictable colors) and a potential time-saver from doing manual work.

Let's start with how conversion can confuse: run the sample project on the iPhone 5s simulator. As this older device doesn't support color management, you'll see weird colors in the simulator's Asset Tests (FIG 4.3). At the same time, the UIImage tests look fine—what gives?

As Xcode compiles the ColorTest images in the asset catalog, the software knows the iPhone 5s doesn't have color management and needs sRGB, so it converts the colors in the PNG files. The JPEG files remain unmodified and look wrong, because iOS ignores the profile. The PNG files appear correctly on screen, because they're no longer the files you put in the catalog.

You *can* use this automatic conversion to your advantage. If you specify a single, high-quality asset like 16-bit Display P3, Xcode will convert it to sRGB during your build. You're free from doing it by hand in Photoshop!

Unfortunately, this approach has a catch: the only way to see the results of Xcode's conversion is to run the app and view the results on screen, each time. You have no way to say, "Show me all the PNG files in the app I just built." If you target many devices, scales, and sizes, you'll launch a lot of simulators to do quality assurance.

And as you saw with Photoshop's Convert to Profile, the raw color values in your image will shift during the build. To ensure these assets match other elements in your interface, you must

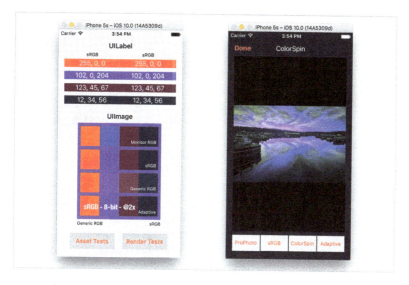

**FIG 4.3:** The UIImage samples (left) appear correct, but the simulator's profiles (right) are a different story.

specify Display P3 in code or the storyboard. UIColor is smart and will apply the same conversion Xcode did in the build.

If you're considering this technique, check out the sample project's Harbor_Universal asset as an example (see -setAdaptiveImage: in AssetViewController.m). You'll likely want to limit automatic conversion to new development, as existing code and storyboards make a lot of assumptions about sRGB.

## Adapting images to displays

On the other hand, you might skip Xcode's automatic conversion, and opt for finer control: creating individual files for the sRGB and Display P3 slots, as you would with the 1x, 2x, and 3x slots for multiple resolutions. This scenario is similar to responsive color for the web—great news if you need to share assets between your website and mobile app.

When you run your app, Xcode will select images from the catalog based on a device's capabilities. Just as an @2x image will load for a Retina display, a 16-bit PNG file loads on a device that supports Display P3. Otherwise, you'll see the normal sRGB file. (This is also how Chapter 3's color-gamut media query works.)

See this for yourself by running the sample app on an actual iPhone 7 or iPad Pro (9.7-inch). You'll see how rich the colors appear—the red and purple colors depict the most change because they're at the extremes of the sRGB gamut. In the Asset Tests, both the ProPhoto and Adaptive samples show a sunset with a wider range of colors (especially with orange).

If you don't have one of these fancy new screens, track what's happening via the iPhone 7 simulator: "Display P3 - 16-bit" denotes when adaptive images appear in the bottom UIImage test and the Adaptive example in Asset Tests. If you run the sample on an older iPhone, you'll see "sRGB - 8-bit" instead.

At this point, you may think these extra resources will make your app download humongous. Luckily, the app-thinning feature introduced in iOS 9 removes unneeded resources before sending everything to the customer's device. The iPhone 7 receives the new wider images, while an iPhone 6s only loads the traditional images.

## RUNNING YOUR APP

Now that your app is running, remember all devices won't handle your images the same way. You may see color shifts on devices that don't support color profiles (iPhone 5s), while other devices (iPhone SE) will display images perfectly (FIG 4.4).

Without support for ProPhoto, the iPhone 5s defaults to sRGB, and the colors become dull and muted. (The earlier ColorSpin example in FIG 4.3 is admittedly a more extreme case of how colors can get mixed up without color management—but it does happen.) It's crucial to note that prior to iOS 9.3, all devices could not manage color.

What decides if a device is capable of enabling color management? The *Graphics Processing Unit* (GPU)! GPUs in mobile

**FIG 4.4:** The iPhone 5s (left) doesn't support color management, the iPhone SE (center) does, and an adaptive image (right) fixes the problem on iPhone 5s.

devices have advanced rapidly. Starting with the A8 chips introduced in the iPhone 6, these processing units have had enough computing power to convert colors. (This line of chips is sometimes called "GPU Family 2." For a full list of devices that support A8 and up, check the iOS Device Compatibility Reference.)

## Changing your view

Just as you did on the web, your mobile app can check if you're running on a P3 screen. For instance, you can define the red, green, and blue values in a UIColor as sRGB or Display P3, and you'll want to pick the ones that match your graphic. Or, maybe you're loading images over a network connection: the request to your server could include a parameter that tells the server to return a version with wider color.

Every UIViewController has a collection of traits, such as the interface idiom, display scale, and size class. These traits define the current environment for your user interface, and any view controller can use the displayGamut property to check if wide color is available:

```
UITraitCollection *traitCollection =
  self.traitCollection;
if (traitCollection.displayGamut ==
  UIDisplayGamutP3) {
  // current display is P3
}
else {
  // current display is sRGB or unspecified
}
```

To create colors in the new gamut, you'll use a variation on a trusty (older) method. Instead of colorWith Red:green:blue:alpha:, create a UIColor with colorWith DisplayP3Red:green:blue:alpha:. For instance, the sample app generates a fully saturated red for a background label with this code:

```
[UIColor colorWithDisplayP3Red:1.0 green:0.0
  blue:0.0 alpha:1.0];
```

On a display without a wider gamut, this code converts colors to sRGB. This automatic conversion process is identical to the one used on assets, so color matches between your images and UIColor are maintained.

To see how this plays out, check the sample project's ViewController.m—the same code adjusts the label's background colors when the view loads.

## Rendering images

Data graphs, social network avatars, photo thumbnails: many of the images we use in our apps are *not* in the asset catalog. These graphics are created at runtime from a variety of user inputs, and you'll need to consider color management as you annotate, transform, and filter these pixels.

The sample ColorfulMobile app includes Render Tests you can access from the main screen. We'll do a quick overview of APIs old and new. (For more details, see the comments in the source code of **RenderViewController.m**, again in the sample project.)

Since iOS 4, the power combo of UIGraphicsBeginImage-Context, UIGraphicsGetImageFromCurrentImageContext, and UIGraphicsEndImageContext has generated dynamic images. Any code you've written in the past will continue to work as you adopt color management in iOS 10, but you'll soon stumble on a problem. These functions only support drawing in 8-bit sRGB: with no support for wide color, your app is going to look pretty dull on the newer screens.

Instead, check out UIGraphicsImageRenderer, a new block-based API, to create UIImage objects that match the screen's resolution and depth. For example, you can generate a 200-point red square in Display P3 like so:

```
const CGSize size = { 200.0, 200.0 };
UIGraphicsImageRenderer *renderer =
  [[UIGraphicsImageRenderer alloc]
  initWithSize:size];
UIImage *image =
  [renderer
  imageWithActions:^(UIGraphicsImageRendererContext
  *context) {
  [[UIColor colorWithDisplayP3Red:1.0 green:0.0
  blue:0.0 alpha:1.0] set];
  [context fillRect:context.format.bounds];
}];
self.imageView.image = image;
```

The first two buttons in the Render Tests show how your code will change. "Draw Old" is implemented the old-fashioned way in -setDrawOld:, while "Draw New" uses the newer techniques in -setDrawNew:. But as soon as you run the code on an sRGB screen, you'll wonder why you bothered: no visual difference exists between the old and new rendering code.

You'll understand why once you load the app on an iPhone 7. The colors achieved with the new image renderer are striking. Unfortunately, since you're reading this in a narrower gamut, I can only convey the relative differences via photo (**FIG 4.5**).

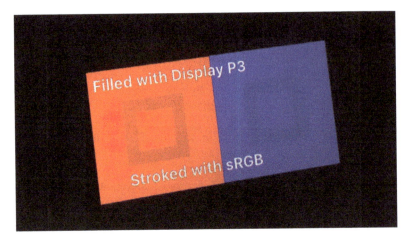

**FIG 4.5:** This photograph of the "Draw New" test on a 9.7-inch iPad Pro shows a dull sRGB box drawn on a bright Display P3 background.

## Matching colors

When using `UIGraphicsImageRenderer` for wide color, your main challenge is getting the colors in code to match your assets as the screen depth changes. The "Colors Wrong" and "Colors Correct" rendering tests demonstrate the importance of choosing the right colors as you draw your assets.

Since images in the asset catalog can be either sRGB or Display P3, you need to watch for a few things:

- If you're drawing on an asset, the colors in the rendering context need to match the image's color space. You'll notice a color shift if you use sRGB to put a red rectangle on top of the same color in a Display P3 image—like with the swatches drawn on ColorTest.
- Update any colors that surround the asset. For example, the purple background that showcases the color strips in the ColorTest assets must change along with the display's gamut.
- The techniques to get an exact color match depend on whether you're using a universal image with automatic

conversion (ColorTest-Universal) or adaptive images (ColorTest-Adaptive). See both approaches in the sample code.

Again, these color shifts are difficult or impossible to see in the simulator. You won't realize you have a visual bug until you run the app on a device with a Display P3 screen.

As you're working with the extended color range in iOS 10, you may see a message like this in your debugging log: "UIColor created with component values far outside the expected range." This is your tip you're trying for a color that's out of gamut and likely to lead to an unwanted color shift. To find out where this is happening, set a symbolic breakpoint on UIColorBreakForOutOfRangeColorComponents and check the call stack when your app stops. (Learn more about setting up symbolic breakpoints with this guide from Big Nerd Ranch.)

## Converting images

Let's loop back to a member of the old power combo, UIGraphicsBeginImageContextWithOptions, which offers parameters for controlling the opacity and scale of the resulting image. The image renderer upstart adds another parameter: prefersExtendedRange.

This extended-range parameter lets you control the color space of the converted image. By default, the image will use the same color space as the display, but sometimes you'll want to use a narrower gamut. The "Modify Image" rendering test shows one such case: generating thumbnail images.

Wider images take up twice as much memory than the ones we've used in the past. Each pixel in a traditional image uses four 8-bit integers for red, green, blue, and alpha. In a wide image, each deeper pixel uses a 16-bit floating-point value for the same data. If you're generating a lot of small images like thumbnails or avatars, that extra memory adds up. Your customer is unlikely to notice the benefits of wide color here, but they'll definitely notice a crash when your app runs out of memory. Save wide color for where it'll have the most visual effect: large areas with rich detail, like photographs.

Another neat feature of the image renderer is its ability to generate PNG and JPEG files with embedded color profiles. This gives you an easy way to create images that can be cached locally or uploaded to a network.

### True Tone

Color management on iOS enables a key feature on some devices: True Tone.

The iPad Pro (9.7-inch) has an ambient light sensor built into the bezel of the screen that detects changes in your viewing environment. (Unfortunately, this feature is absent on the iPhone 7, presumably because the smaller form factor can't spare space for the sensor.)

iOS periodically checks the sensor and adjusts the profile of the display dynamically (based on the "white point" of the screen) so colors are more natural and reading stays comfortable.

For most apps, this constant adjustment is welcome and will make your app look better without extra effort on your part. Some apps, such as games or photo editors, may want to lessen the color-shifting effect by using `UIWhitePointAdaptivity-Style` in the `Info.plist` configuration.

To get an idea of how True Tone works, take an iPad Pro into a dark room and compare the white background in Photos with the same color in Safari. When you're viewing images, `UIWhitePointAdaptivityStylePhoto` makes the True Tone effect much less pronounced than the warmer colors in the web browser.

## DO I REALLY NEED TO DO THIS?

No one likes to rewrite code that's working just fine. Even the engineers at Apple.

But the changes we're seeing in iOS are wide ranging: everything from the pixel formats in Core Graphics to the way Photos displays an image. This huge level of work is a clear indicator that Apple sees color management as a crucial part of their platform. It's more than likely other platforms, including Android, will follow Apple's lead—I suspect it won't be long before wide color is available on all new devices.

As these new devices proliferate, *a lot* of content *won't* be in sRGB. Remember that as of iOS 10, the camera takes photos in Display P3 for maximum quality. These images, in turn, will pass onto your app for editing, your server for storage, and your network for sharing.

To understand the scale of this change, note that in 2013 over 1.2 billion phones were taking pictures, a number that grew exponentially. In 2015, Apple sold over 26,000 phones per hour—and now those iPhones have wide color.

Adopting color management in your app won't be easy. You're going to find drawing code that's hard to update. Development tools are still evolving and may not be fully compatible with color management. Testing your code is also more difficult than it was with Retina displays: you can't just run your app at two or three times normal size. You need a display that can show a wider range of color, which is currently limited to the latest Retina iMac, an iPad Pro, and the latest iPhone.

But obstacles like these never get in the way of developers who want their apps to look the very best. My advice is to focus your efforts on the parts of your app where vibrant content has the biggest payoff—both you and your customers will be impressed with how much accurate color improves the experience.

# 5

# DESKTOP APPS

YOUR IOS APP is a hit! Customers are craving a desktop version and you've created a new project in Xcode to build a Mac app. Let's examine color considerations on this platform. (Fortunately, after the in-depth changes for the web and mobile, this chapter will be quick!)

As you did in Chapter 4, download a sample app, Colorful, to follow along and do your own experiments—you'll also see it in the screenshots.

## ANYTHING GOES

After seeing so many platforms that dictate a color space, we're now on an OS with no limits: your Mac displays any color space you choose (**FIG 5.1**).

The growing pains of iOS are bygones on macOS—Apple built ColorSync into the operating system's first release in 2001, making color management ubiquitous on the desktop.

You're also not limited to just one color space: multiple spaces can be mixed and matched as necessary. Any one of the choices from the color picker's gear menu is valid and will show up correctly at all points in the development process.

Like the rest of macOS, Xcode displays images using embedded color profiles, so make sure other controls in your interface have the same profile. For example, compare the test images created from ColorTest.psd with the Generic RGB and sRGB label-background colors in the sample project (**FIG 5.2**).

## RESTRAINT IS IN ORDER

In spite of this newfound flexibility, you'll still want to be careful about how you use color in a Mac app.

Sometimes sticking with the system's default color space will make your development smoother. In other cases, your job will be easier if you use a common color space between your mobile and desktop apps. Let's look at your options.

**FIG 5.1:** Interface Builder for macOS displays (123, 45, 67) in whatever color space you select in the picker.

**FIG 5.2:** A Mac app using many color spaces simultaneously.

**The default color**

The AppKit framework to create Mac apps has traditionally used "calibrated" colors. This is just another term for Generic RGB, so if you want to create an NSColor in this color space, use colorWithCalibratedRed:green:blue:alpha:.

This de facto standard appears in a lot of our tools. Many developers, including your humble author, used the standard color picker numerous times before they noticed it had a gear icon to change profiles. Managed color is everywhere you look on your Mac, but that hasn't stopped any of us from creating apps without worrying about color spaces.

## Common color

If you're developing an app for macOS as well as the web or iOS, working with sRGB color can make your life way easier. Cross-platform apps typically share a lot of assets: you'll spend less time making graphics and achieve a more consistent interface if you build everything in one color space.

To use sRGB in your controls, select it from the color picker's gear menu while entering your red, green, and blue component values. In the sample Colorful project, the NSText-Field background colors on the right-hand side demonstrate this approach.

If you need to create sRGB colors in code, you have two choices:

```
[NSColor colorWithSRGBRed:(123.0/255.0)
   green:(45.0/255.0) blue:(67.0/255.0) alpha:1.0];
```

Or:

```
[NSColor colorWithRed:(123.0/255.0)
   green:(45.0/255.0) blue:(67.0/255.0) alpha:1.0];
```

These produce identical results, but the second form makes your life simpler because the name is very similar to its iOS counterpart.

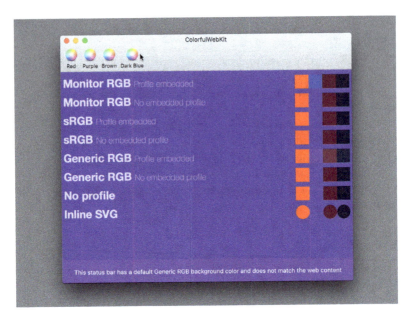

**FIG 5.3:** A color mismatch between WebView and the native controls of a Mac app.

If you have more specific needs, you can create NSColor with any components and color space. For example, if you want to match the iMac's wide-gamut display, use a CGColorRef created with kCGColorSpaceDisplayP3. Check the sample project for details.

## WebView

As we wind up our tour of development platforms, we're back on the web!

Since the introduction of Safari, the Mac has had excellent support for embedding web content in apps. Using the WebKit framework and a WebView object, apps can add HTML, CSS, and JavaScript to the user experience, while integrating with the desktop's unique capabilities.

When you use WebView in your app, you gain the same color management available in Safari. Everything you saw in Chapter 3 remains applicable. Your primary concern is to make sure that assets in the native part of your app match what's in your HTML and CSS (FIG 5.3). Sticking with sRGB is your best bet.

To learn more about ways to deploy WebView in a Mac app, download the ColorfulWebKit sample code. You'll also get a quick taste of the interaction between a native app and a web app.

Desktop apps often take a backseat to web and native apps running on our phones and tablets. Except in one major area: the development tools we use to create those mobile products. As the products we build become more color aware, you can avoid problems by knowing how your desktop tools handle color.

# CONCLUSION

YOU'VE COME A LONG WAY since that first glimpse of Dr. Eyeful's website. Now that the pain has subsided, you're hopefully more comfortable with your tools and the colors they produce. You've also learned how to get predictable results while you work with color on any platform.

If I could offer one piece of advice at the end of this lengthy treatise: learn to love sRGB. It's the safest color space and avoids color shifts stemming from profile mismatches. Adopting this color space also makes saving assets less error prone, and lets you use the same files across a variety of environments.

But don't get *too* attached to sRGB. The displays on our existing devices will change in the coming years, and you'll want to move your workflows to these wider gamuts. The techniques in this book will ease that transition and make your products look even better on a desktop, tablet, or phone.

With the help of color management, your future looks bright!

# ACKNOWLEDGMENTS

Any project that takes years to complete includes the contributions of many people. This book got its start in 2014, when my pals Jeffrey Zeldman and Ethan Marcotte showed enthusiasm for an early draft. That led to an introduction to Katel LeDû who, despite my repeated attempts otherwise, kept this project on track.

Tina Lee is a secret weapon. She finds vast swaths of words that aren't really needed, repairs my abuse of the passive voice, and generally makes me look like a better writer than I am. She'd probably like to get rid of this sentence and the prior one, but she told me I could do anything I want here, and aren't you glad the rest of the book isn't like this?

Work on this book was a constant reminder that I have awesome peers. Pieter Omvlee (Sketch), Tom Giannattasio (Macaw), Wade Cosgrove (Coda), and Simonas Bastys (Pixelmator) helped me understand how their excellent tools manage color. Marc Edwards, Troy Gaul, Gus Mueller, and Daniel Kennett provided excellent feedback on a complicated topic. Steve Troughton-Smith and his huge collection of devices helped with many screenshots. Thanks to you all!

Another group deserves special recognition: the folks at Apple who are leading the way with color management. Their knowledge and thoughtfulness show in videos, email correspondence, and blog posts. You know who you are, and you have my sincere thanks.

As this project neared completion, I sent an unfinished manuscript to Mike Krieger and the team at Instagram. It was a joy to hear that my book not only helped them get ready for iOS 10, but also played a part in their feature during the iPhone 7 keynote. Wow!

The last contribution to this book came from my friend John Gruber. I've been an admirer of his writing since that first fireball many years ago, and it's an honor to have him introduce my own work. :whiskey:

Finally, this whole thing couldn't have happened without Lauren Mayes, who's been by my side every day offering advice, motivation, and love. Thanks, sweetie.

# RESOURCES

See my site for links to this book's sample color tests, Photoshop files, and Xcode projects, all in one spot.

## More about color management

Photographers have been managing colors for years. Learn from folks who've explored how color management affects digital imagery:

- "Color Space and Color Profiles," Richard Anderson and Peter Krogh. From the American Society of Media Photographers. Discusses in depth the methods used to reproduce color in digital photography.
- "Digital-Image Color Spaces," Jeffrey Friedl. A multipart series exploring color spaces in digital images. Note that some of the information about how web browsers and operating systems handle color is outdated.
- "Overview of Color Management," Sean McHugh. An excellent three-part series showing how color management factors into digital photography.
- "Soft Proofing Photos & Prints," Sean McHugh. Explains the details of Photoshop's color-conversion support, including advanced options such as rendering intent and black point compensation.
- "SRGB vs. Adobe RGB 1998," Sean McHugh. Explores the differences between the two most common color spaces in digital photography.
- "The Role of Working Spaces in Adobe Applications" (PDF), Andrew Rodney. A great overview of how Adobe uses color spaces. Covers the origins and features of the options in the Color Settings dialog.

## The web: past, present, and future

Get an idea of how color is evolving on the web:

- "Is Your System ICC Version 4 Ready?," International Color Consortium. Yet another color difference between browsers! A newer version of the ICC profile format is not supported in some browsers, including Chrome and Firefox.
- "Improving Color on the Web," Dean Jackson. This post on the WebKit blog shows all the ways Apple's browser is changing to match improved display technologies.
- "A Standard Default Color Space for the Internet - sRGB," Michael Stokes, Matthew Anderson, Srinivasan Chandrasekar, and Ricardo Motta. Although now obsolete, this original specification for sRGB was the first time many developers encountered color spaces and profiles.
- "CSS Color Module Level 3," W3C. The current CSS color specification.
- "CSS Color Module Level 4," W3C. This draft proposal includes support for color profiles and device-dependent colors. Note the new color() function and @color-profile rule. Although not directly related to color management, color-mod() will be helpful for adjusting colors in a web design.

## Colors and code

Learn from the experiences of Mac developers:

- "Introduction to Color Management Overview," Apple. Oriented toward the Mac, but many of the concepts and techniques now apply to iOS developers as well.
- "Technical Note TN2035: ColorSync on Mac OS X," Apple. Covers all aspects of ColorSync support on Mac OS X. Much of the information also applies to iOS.

## Tools, tools, tools

Color management will become a bigger part of your design and development workflow:

- "Color Management in Your Tools," Craig Hockenberry. A quick overview of how various design and development tools manage color.

Developers have special needs when it comes to picking colors. These free tools integrate with the standard color picker and let you output color as code for the web or native apps:

- Developer Color Picker, Panic
- Skala Color, Bjango
- xScope, The Iconfactory. This developer tool was the genesis for this book. It does a lot of things besides color too.

## The gory details

Dive into the fascinating intricacies—terms and mathematics—of color science:

- "iPhone 6 Pixels," Bryan Jones. The way displays are manufactured affects how they display color. This retinal neuroscientist looks at various screens from Apple underneath a microscope.
- Planckian Locus. That weird curved shape you've seen throughout the book has a name, and it lies at the heart of the physics behind the electromagnetic radiation that reaches our eye.
- Trichromacy. Red, green, and blue. It comes down to light-sensitive proteins in our cone cells. This Wikipedia page is a great place to start learning more about the biology of our vision and how our retina responds to light.

## Specifications

Explore the standards behind color management:

- "Introduction to the ICC Profile Format," International Color Consortium
- "Embedding ICC Profiles in Standard Image File Formats," International Color Consortium
- Adobe RGB specification (PDF), Adobe
- sRGB specification (PDF), International Color Consortium

# REFERENCES

Shortened URLs are numbered sequentially; the related long URLs are listed below for reference.

## Introduction

00-01 http://xscopeapp.com/

## Chapter 1

01-01 https://developer.apple.com/library/content/releasenotes/MacOSX/
WhatsNewInOSX/Articles/MacOSX10_11_2.html#//apple_ref/doc/uid/
TP40016630-SW1

01-02 http://www.macrumors.com/2015/10/16/new-4k-imac-teardown/

01-03 http://xscopeapp.com/

## Chapter 2

02-01 http://furbo.org/color/Downloads/ColorTest.psd.zip

02-02 https://en.wikipedia.org/wiki/Loudness_war

02-03 http://furbo.org/color/Downloads/ColorTest-sRGB.psd.zip

02-04 http://furbo.org/color/Downloads/ColorTest-GenericRGB.psd.zip

02-05 https://developer.apple.com/library/mac/qa/qa1430/_index.html

02-06 http://furbo.org/color/Downloads/ColorTest-MonitorRGB.png.zip

02-07 http://furbo.org/color/Downloads/Image-ProPhoto.jpg

02-08 http://www.dpbestflow.org/color/color-space-and-color-profiles

02-09 https://fstoppers.com/pictures/adobergb-vs-srgb-3167

02-10 https://blogs.adobe.com/crawlspace/2015/06/save-for-web-in-photo-
shop-cc-2015.html

02-11 https://helpx.adobe.com/photoshop/using/export-artboards-layers.html

02-12 https://helpx.adobe.com/photoshop/how-to/design-with-artboards.html

02-13 http://furbo.org/color/Tools/

## Chapter 3

03-01 http://www.w3.org/TR/css3-color/#rgb-color

03-02 https://www.w3.org/Graphics/Color/sRGB.html

03-03 http://www.w3.org/TR/SVG/color.html#ColorIntroduction

03-04    https://www.w3.org/TR/SVG/refs.html#ref-ICC42

03-05    https://www.w3.org/TR/SVG/painting.html#SpecifyingPaint

03-06    https://html.spec.whatwg.org/multipage/scripting.html
#colour-spaces-and-colour-correction

03-07    http://furbo.org/color/CanvasTest/

03-08    https://github.com/whatwg/html/issues/299

03-09    http://furbo.org/color/Colorful/

03-10    https://webkit.org/blog/73/color-spaces/

03-11    http://furbo.org/color/Colorful/

03-12    https://bugs.chromium.org/p/chromium/issues/detail?id=44872

03-13    https://www.w3.org/TR/css3-color/#dropped

03-14    http://blogs.windows.com/bloggingwindows/2015/03/30/introducing-
project-spartan-the-new-browser-built-for-windows-10/

03-15    http://www.apple.com/ipad-pro/

03-16    https://jeffcarlson.com/2016/04/21/the-9-7-inch-ipad-pro-color-gamut/

03-17    http://furbo.org/color/Downloads/Image-ProPhoto.jpg

03-18    https://drafts.csswg.org/mediaqueries-4/#color-gamut

03-19    http://caniuse.com/#feat=picture

03-20    http://furbo.org/color/ResponsiveColor/

03-21    http://furbo.org/color/WideGamut

03-22    https://imageoptim.com/

03-23    http://furbo.org/color/Colorful/

## Chapter 4

04-01    https://developer.android.com/reference/android/graphics/Color.html

04-02    https://developer.apple.com/videos/play/wwdc2015/510/

04-03    https://developer.apple.com/videos/play/wwdc2016/712/

04-04    https://developer.apple.com/videos/play/wwdc2016/501/

04-05    http://furbo.org/color/downloads/ColorfulMobile.zip

04-06    https://developer.apple.com/xcode/

04-07    https://developer.apple.com/library/content/documentation/IDEs/
Conceptual/AppDistributionGuide/AppThinning/AppThinning.html

04-08    https://developer.apple.com/library/content/documentation/
DeviceInformation/Reference/iOSDeviceCompatibility/
HardwareGPUInformation/HardwareGPUInformation.html#//apple_ref/
doc/uid/TP40013599-CH106-SW1

04-09    https://www.bignerdranch.com/blog/xcode-breakpoint-wizardry/

04-10  http://petapixel.com/2015/04/09/this-is-what-the-history-of-camera-sales-looks-like-with-smartphones-included/

04-11  http://om.co/2016/01/27/what-in-2015-apple-sold-how-many-million-iphones/

# Chapter 5

05-01  http://furbo.org/color/Downloads/Colorful.zip
05-02  http://furbo.org/color/Downloads/ColorfulWebKit.zip

# Resources

06-01  http://www.dpbestflow.org/color/color-space-and-color-profiles
06-02  http://regex.info/blog/photo-tech/color-spaces-page1
06-03  http://www.cambridgeincolour.com/tutorials/color-management1.htm
06-04  http://www.cambridgeincolour.com/tutorials/color-spaces.htm
06-05  http://www.cambridgeincolour.com/tutorials/color-space-conversion.htm
06-06  http://www.cambridgeincolour.com/tutorials/soft-proofing.htm
06-07  http://www.cambridgeincolour.com/tutorials/sRGB-AdobeRGB1998.htm
06-08  https://www.adobe.com/digitalimag/pdfs/phscs2ip_colspace.pdf
06-09  http://www.color.org/version4html.xalter
06-10  https://webkit.org/blog/6682/improving-color-on-the-web/
06-11  https://www.w3.org/Graphics/Color/sRGB
06-12  https://www.w3.org/TR/css3-color/
06-13  https://drafts.csswg.org/css-color/#changes
06-14  https://developer.apple.com/library/mac/documentation/GraphicsImaging/Conceptual/csintro/csintro_intro/csintro_intro.html
06-15  https://developer.apple.com/library/mac/technotes/tn2035/_index.html
06-16  http://furbo.org/color/Tools/
06-17  http://download.panic.com/picker/
06-18  https://bjango.com/mac/skalacolor/
06-19  http://xscopeapp.com
06-20  http://prometheus.med.utah.edu/~bwjones/2014/10/iphone-6-pixels/
06-21  https://en.wikipedia.org/wiki/Planckian_locus
06-22  https://en.wikipedia.org/wiki/Trichromacy
06-23  http://www.color.org/iccprofile.xalter
06-24  http://www.color.org/profile_embedding.xalter
06-25  https://www.adobe.com/digitalimag/pdfs/AdobeRGB1998.pdf
06-26  http://www.color.org/specification/ICC1v43_2010-12.pdf

# INDEX

## ABOUT A BOOK APART

We cover the emerging and essential topics in web design and development with style, clarity, and above all, brevity—because working designer-developers can't afford to waste time.

## COLOPHON

The text is set in FF Yoga and its companion, FF Yoga Sans, both by Xavier Dupré. Headlines and cover are set in Titling Gothic by David Berlow.

## ABOUT THE AUTHOR

**Craig Hockenberry** has been making software since 1976 and built his first website at 14.4 kilobits per second. He's a principal at the Iconfactory, a company that's been changing the face of our computers for over twenty years. His writing has helped many fellow developers in their work, and that makes him happy. So does a Manhattan.

www.ingramcontent.com/pod-product-compliance
Lightning Source LLC
LaVergne TN
LVHW012333060326
832902LV00011B/1860